Ft. Worth

Jan. '76

FREEDOM—VICTORY—LOVE
ACCEPTANCE—PURPOSE

The big words of life take on a new meaning for the people in these pages when each gives control of his life to God.

Inside this book you meet a tripped-out
go-go dancer,
see marriages on the brink of divorce,
watch confused teens,
listen in on a 4 A.M. phone call, and
touch the vacuum of rejection, depression
and loneliness no human can fill.

The loving touch of KBIQ "People Who Care" begins a healing process in each person which leads to Jesus Christ and . . .

FREEDOM—VICTORY—LOVE
ACCEPTANCE—PURPOSE

To Al
With all our love
& His too
Marjie Thompson
Mickie Rogers

God...
where are you?

by Mickie Rogers and Marjie Thompson

Foreword by Peter Gillquist

A Division of G/L Publications
Glendale, California, U.S.A.

© Copyright 1971 by G/L Publications
Printed in U.S.A.

Published by
Regal Books Division, G/L Publications
Glendale, California 91209, U.S.A.

Library of Congress Catalog Card No. 76-152101
Hard-cover edition: ISBN 0-8307-0102-8
Paperback edition: ISBN 0-8307-0100-1

DEDICATION

To our God who cares
Because He does
We do

Contents

Foreword

Lord Chesterton said once, "If it's complicated, it's wrong."

On that basis, Mickie Rogers and Marjie Thompson are "right on." They have gotten under the skins of people who have found a lovely walk with God, and they have told of these experiences with simplicity and a hominess that makes you want to get to know the folks of whom they write.

Of course, this is not the first time that the personal experiences of individuals and their Lord have been told. But what grabbed me is that these men and women are, for the most part, my friends, my neighbors and even *me!* They are not celebrities, professional athletes, political leaders, actors and actresses or prominent success stories from the business world. They are just people.

And, even more importantly, they are not professional Christians whose testimonies are so often accented with how many hours a day they have come to spend in Bible reading and prayer, or in how many souls they point to Christ per annum.

If the reader-to-be is looking for some quick answers to spirituality, a short course in heavy theology, or biblical advice on current moral dilemmas, look on! It's not here!

But if you would like to peek into some people's lives . . . people who are short on money at the end of the month, who have wondered if they *really* loved their marriage partners, who have had unwanted kids, who wish they hadn't moved from the last place they lived . . . and find out how *they* met Jesus Christ and began seeing their lives reprogrammed, then *GOD . . . Where Are You?* will give you great joy. The God of whom they speak is so accessible and knowable.

And could it be that the Lord will use what He is doing in Seattle to germinate ideas for similar modes of meeting people and their needs in other parts of this country and the world?

I've found Jesus extremely sufficient today. Tomorrow should be even better!

Peter E. Gillquist
Memphis, Tennessee

Introduction

But God had a better idea!

KBIQ was born on December 1, 1967, with a new sound, a new format and a new purpose. Until then KGFM, the forerunner of the new station, had lived its life in obscurity broadcasting Christian music to the Christian world. Not a bad idea, but what about all those people out there in the world who were looking for meaning, purpose and order to their lives? People who were seeking answers to the questions, "Who am I? Why am I here? Where am I going? Does anyone care?"

A group of people were concerned about the ones out there asking these questions. They had found the Answer and couldn't keep Him to themselves. The reality they had found in their own lives was sufficient to cause them to want to broadcast the "good news."

Thus the seeds were planted and KGFM was buried. In its place KBIQ with its logo, the sound of a thundering jet roaring across living rooms in full stereo, captured the attention of the people who were asking life-shaking questions.

KBIQ became known as the contemporary sound of music in the Pacific Northwest. "From Vancouver (British Columbia) to Vancouver (Washington), the most powerful FM station in the Northwest."

"You're in the giant reach of stereo 105—comforting, isn't it?" KBIQ quickly began an upward swing in the ratings and was heard in many Seattle area department stores, restaurants, barber shops, dentist's offices, taverns, homes and car radios.

Along with the listenable music came the subtle, catchy "God commercials." Ears perked up with surprise, then the thirty-second spot would be over. Listeners unconsciously found themselves waiting for the next little message. They might hear a dialogue like this:

"You know those people who started the rumor that God is dead?"

"Yeah."

"He loves them too."

"Hmmm, that's some God!"

After a few months the listener was introduced to a telephone number which would put him in touch with "People Who Care."

"If you would like to know how Christ can relate to your life in this practical way, call 546-6551.

'People Who Care' are standing by to talk with you and you can call right now."

Listeners gradually began to respond, though often a little reticently. At first some would hang up at the surprise of hearing a real live voice instead of the recorded message they might have expected. But thirteen men and women who call themselves "People Who Care" were on hand to listen and to share their own "life content" with the caller.

In the pages of this book you will encounter some of those who have responded to "People Who Care." A woman sitting alone in quiet desperation. A man blinded in an accident attempting suicide. A drug addict alone and helpless. A young couple, quarrelling, on the edge of divorce. A housewife simply looking for some kind of meaning to the mundane routine of her life.

You will meet a variety of personalities. Some who have called out of desperation, others from sheer boredom, but none whose lives haven't been altered in a fascinating way.

You will be introduced to some of the "People Who Care": businessmen, a telephone repairman, an interior designer, a Boeing employee, housewives, nurses and former youth workers. These are men and women whose own lives have been enriched through the opportunity they have had of watching a mighty God at work in the lives of their fellow man.

1

God, Where Are You?

"I would like to find out how I can know God personally," Cindy stated simply, after her call had been channeled to one of the "People Who Care." Cindy, who was only thirteen then, is an extremely sensitive and highly intellectual girl. To say the least, she is a challenge for any adult of average intelligence.

Cindy had called "People Who Care" six months earlier. At that time she was looking for proof for the existence of God. She had been through catechism and the religious routine. At the age of ten she had discarded many of her earlier teachings concerning religion as irrelevent to her own life. She had questioned many of the things she was

1

being taught and had not received answers that satisfied her. She found so many discrepancies they only confused her.

When she called the first time she was told simply that God's existence cannot be proven by intellectual means. The real proof is in the life He gives to the individual who would choose to trust Him.

Cindy had since pondered the contradictions she was growing up with these past few months. In junior high school she was taught that God was someone man had created to fill a need in his own life. These ideas disturbed her immensely. In her heart dwelt a sense of restlessness, an awareness of a presence that she was unable to rationalize away through her intellect.

Cindy spent a lot of her time alone in her room, as most teenagers do, listening to rock music. Now and then she liked a change of pace and she stumbled on KBIQ one night when she was tired of the heavy beat. It became a habit for her to switch on KBIQ periodically. She kept hearing those spots that said things like, "You can know Him personally. You can experience the love of God. He is the great problem solver." If there were even a remote possibility that there could be some truth in what she kept hearing, Cindy wanted to find out.

They met then, over a soda, Cindy and that "Someone Who Cared." Through the clamor of the beating of drums and "happy birthday" choruses at Farrell's Ice-Cream Parlor, Cindy learned of God's love and concern for her.

Her capacious green eyes opened wider and a smile occasionally began to break through her

2

somber countenance as she started to see that Jesus Christ was a real person, alive today. He was some-one who loved Cindy and had already provided for her the way to know God personally. She listened eagerly. Every now and then she slowly pushed back a lock of long straight blonde hair.

Cindy was full of questions. She was relieved to learn that Christianity was really not a religion as she had always been taught but a spontaneous re-lationship with Jesus Christ. This relationship was not based on Cindy's performance but on love and trust.

Her parents had been divorced when she was nine. She loved them both a lot and had resented the break-up which had left her alone with her mother. It was a difficult period of adjustment for both Cindy and her mother. Her mother tried to the best of her ability to be both mother and father to her only child. The added demands of a job took her away from home much more than she wanted to be.

Cindy resented the household responsibilities she was called upon to shoulder. She began to resent her mother and found she could blame her for much that was happening.

Cindy's resentment grew into hatred for her mother. The atmosphere between them became more and more tense as hostility deepened. Com-munications were at an all-time low. Cindy had felt rejected and insecure, yet was mature in many ways far beyond her thirteen years.

Her maturity and spiritual understanding pre-sented still another problem. She was unable to

3

find Christian companionship. She discovered that very few of her peers took God seriously. Few were even remotely interested in discovering Him. All too painfully the shock of learning that she lived in a post-Christian culture left her with many questions unanswered. Her trust in Christ began to waver and she began once again to rely on her own finite decisions.

As problems and tensions increased at home, she began to dream of living with her father. She had an unusual attachment for him and finally convinced herself that everything would be "super-cool" if she could just be with him. She began to work the situation until at last her father agreed to take her, even against the protests of her new stepmother.

Though her father loved her and tried his best, Cindy experienced the resentment and rejection of her stepmother. Cindy's presence seemed to create a wedge. It was almost as though the two of them were competing for the love of the only man in the house. Cindy's grades began to go down. She started missing school and spending whole days at home alone in her room. Melancholy evolved into depression and soon Cindy was a ninth-grade drop-out.

Her depression increased and her desire to live decreased. She felt unloved and unwanted. Out of desperation Cindy swallowed part of a bottle of sleeping pills. It was not quite enough to end her life but enough to cause her father to sit up and take notice. He placed her under psychiatric care.

In the hospital her days were kept occupied with

creative projects, doctors' appointments and other activities such as TV, Ping-Pong and daily group therapy sessions. All in all, to Cindy it was boring and she felt trapped. She didn't seem to be getting better.

At the end of five weeks she still found herself faced with the hopelessness of her situation. Depression and long crying spells occupied the greater part of many of her days.

Amidst the overwhelming problems that had faced Cindy these past few months God had faded into the background. She had had no contact with any Christians except her grandmother but Cindy thought of her as a fanatic. Grandma certainly seemed happy even through many hardships and trials.

"One day," Cindy recalled, "When I was really depressed and looking for some way to end the whole thing, I remembered some things about God. As though He was standing right there I began to talk to Him and ask for help. Almost immediately the depression left. I thought once again about 'People Who Care.' Nearly a year had passed since that day at Farrell's Ice-Cream Parlor. I thought once again about the love of God and the way I had felt a year ago when I began to experience the life He gives. Somehow I knew that the answer was to get back to God. The question was: How?"

Cindy called information, then dialed the "People Who Care" number hopefully. She was immediately put in touch with the same person who had met with her a year before. "She was so happy to hear from me that I was more convinced than ever that those people really did care," Cindy said. "She had written to me when I was living with my father, but I hadn't answered. I had been too depressed to communicate with anyone."

Now once again Cindy began to experience the reality of God's presence as she was reminded that He still loved her and that Christ was still in her life, though she hadn't been aware of His presence there.

Cindy was full of a lot of questions and doubts. The only people she knew that were Christians were those "People Who Care" and her grandmother. Her intellect often got in the way of her trust in Christ.

Then a new patient in the hospital began to talk to Cindy about Christ. She seemed radiant and she said many of the same things Cindy had heard from the "People Who Care." This was a real encouragement to Cindy and she and Pam had some great times of sharing together.

Cindy's periods of depression gradually began to be replaced by hope as she found herself wanting to get to know Christ better.

Soon she discovered the hatred she had had for her mother began to be replaced by understanding and compassion. She called her mother occasionally, whenever hospital rules would permit. "As I began to understand that mother's life hasn't been easy my antipathy for her started to disappear," Cindy said. "There are still problems but now at least we can talk without having a 'yell-in'."

Cindy is very much aware that her circumstances may continue to be difficult. There is still the prob-

6

lem of where she will live and the problem of finding Christian companionship. But today Cindy is more confident than ever before that with Christ in control of her life, together they can have dominion over the circumstances.

She is gradually learning that she needs to leave the decision making in the hands of Him who knows the beginning from the end and desires the best life has to offer her.

2

I've Been There

When I was fifteen my mother bought a bus ticket for me and I left New Orleans in the middle of the night.

From the time I was two years old, I was shuffled back and forth between my divorced parents and my grandmother.

Mom had been keeping house for a white man. Jobs were hard to find and she didn't want to take any chance of losing hers. So when I complained to her about his always touching and pinching me, she solved the problem by sending me away.

That incident was the beginning of what was to become a growing and deep-seated hatred of whites.

In California I started running with a wild

bunch. I met a girl who was going with a sailor and she introduced me to one of his buddies. They bought rum and Coke and picked us up every day after school.

One night we went to Long Beach and really got loaded. He took me to his garage apartment and asked me if I knew how to take care of myself. I said sure. I didn't want him to think I was stupid, but I honestly didn't know what he was talking about. Then I was afraid if I didn't play the game I would lose my sailor and going with a sailor was no small matter.

By the time I found out I was pregnant, the sailor had shipped out to Hong Kong. He was notified by the chaplain of my condition. I was sure he would want to marry me because I thought he cared so much for me. Instead, he let me know that if he were forced to marry me that I would spend the rest of my life regretting it. I never saw him again.

When the baby was a few months old I got a job in Los Angeles. I met Del, who was part white and part Indian. We were married within three weeks and had two blissful years of marriage. Our baby girl was born during this time.

But there was a wedge being driven between us. One of his close friends invited us to his apartment for coffee. I glanced at an open drawer in the kitchen. It was bulging with letters with a current date addressed to my husband. I read several. Some were from his mother. Others were from his girl, wanting to know when she could come to California so they could be married.

Del hadn't found the courage to tell his family or friends he had married a black girl. He knew they would disapprove.

Our marriage started going downhill. Gradually, like a cancer lying dormant, then suddenly becoming malignant, my hatred for whites was rekindled. Nothing Del could say or do would convince me that he didn't look down on me.

Self-pity became my chief pastime. I started going out when Del was at work. I wasn't legally old enough to drink but I spent a lot of time in bars. I just sat there and cried.

I met a man in the bar who seemed sympathetic. When I unloaded on him he said, "That's what happens when girls like you marry white guys. Why don't you just leave him?" His reaction only served to deepen and justify in my own eyes the self-pity that was swallowing me. He said he would treat me like a lady if I went out with him. I remembered going to his place, but that's all I remembered. When I left he told me I had been there two days.

Del and I stuck it out together through the birth of a third child, even though neither of us knew for certain who the father was. The wall between us grew higher and higher. I harbored bitterness and contempt for Del and my hatred for whites deepened.

In a final attempt at saving the marriage, Del took me to Alaska to meet his mother and stepfather. He was sure that when I met with their approval everything would work out.

Until then I had never really known what rejection was. His stepfather wouldn't even sit at the same table with me. In Ketchikan, to my own surprise, blacks and whites walk down one side of the street together, and the Indians take the other. I knew about Indians, but I didn't know they were lower on the totem pole—their own—than we were.

The first day with this group was like a nightmare. I watched in disbelief as his mother cooked the evening meal for the family of eighteen. She took potatoes from a huge bin and dumped them unpeeled into a large porcelain kettle, dirt and all. She served baked halibut heads, one apiece, about the size of a baseball, and a big bowl of lime-green seaweed. I sat nauseated, staring at my plate, the huge eyes of the fish staring back at me, the grey potatoes in a bed of gravel, the slimy green seaweed. I soon discarded the idea of eating the muddy potatoes. My teeth grating on the gravel gave me goosebumps. I attempted several times to tackle the fish head, but every time I touched it with the fork its mouth opened, teeth still intact. The seaweed was the only hope left of gaining their approval. Never having eaten seaweed I was not aware that it swells when wet. I pushed a large handful in my mouth. It swelled. I couldn't swallow it. I just sat there, my mouth ballooning with the seaweed as eighteen pairs of eyes stared mockingly. I pushed the chair back and ran from the table in tears, knowing well that I had not passed the test.

We stayed in Alaska one miserable year. Del's

11

mother spent the entire summer trying to make an Indian out of me.

Shortly after we learned I was pregnant again, we flew back to California.

My fourth child was born. Del couldn't find a job and we were on welfare. I wondered if it was because of my color. Bitterness began to burn again and I hated him. I felt sick when I looked at him and I couldn't stand to have him touch me.

I began seeing a psychiatrist, but the cancer of bitterness and hatred kept eating away inside of me. When Del could stand it no longer he went to Seattle and found a job.

Desperately searching for love and acceptance, I began "running the streets" and soon I was pregnant for the fifth time. I returned for more psychiatric treatment. I started taking overdoses of pills. One night I took a whole bottle. I woke up in the hospital and Del was standing beside me. He took me back to Seattle.

We thought of giving the baby up, but Del decided it wouldn't be fair to me. Things went well for about two months, until his brother came to visit. His glance fell on each of the five multicolored children, then back to Del. "I don't know about you, you can have more black children. I would never marry no Negro woman, 'cause I would hate to have all these little Negro kids."

The impact of that incident renewed the ugly scars of rejection. Hatred and hostility welled up once again.

I went into long periods of depression. Crying spells became the normal part of every day. Even the psychiatric treatment didn't help to erase the bitterness that continued to eat away.

Utterly discouraged with his own efforts to find a solution, Del called the movers and transported the children and me back to L.A. where my mother was. Meanwhile he filed for divorce.

I met Joe, a black man, and he moved into my apartment. When my divorce was final we were married.

Joe and I got along fine for about a year. We both shared and harbored together an equal antagonism towards whites.

When my oldest son was hospitalized after being struck by a car, Del flew down to see him. Del's short visit triggered a sizzling contempt in Joe, and he went off the deep end. He said, "If you can have your white husband here then I can have my black girl friends." He started running around so I did too.

My mother took the children and Joe and I went our separate ways but sharing the same apartment. I was running the streets again pregnant and swallowing any kind of pill I could get my hands on. I didn't care if I lived or died.

Once again I woke up in the hospital having taken an overdose of drugs, this time in the psychiatric ward. I was released a few days later but was soon back again, this time in o.b.

I moved to a small apartment with the new baby. My other children were with my mother and the baby was all I had to call my own.

When the baby was six weeks old I left her with a baby-sitter down the hall while I went to the

13

doctor. When I returned a few hours later she was gone. After a frantic search that lasted three days, I was to learn that Joe had kidnapped the baby and by then was in Arkansas with his mother. I became hysterical and was again rushed to the hospital in a state of shock.

I began regular visits to a psychiatrist again. He advised me to forget about the baby and get my other children back. I tried to take care of the children but I was like a zombie, seldom eating or sleeping and living on the effects of the drugs I was increasingly consuming.

I wrote to Del and pleaded with him to take me back.

When he found a house he sent for us, and we were married again. This time we had a big wedding.

Outwardly things were looking up. I was able to function without drugs and care for the five children, but I couldn't forget the baby. I'd lay awake nights and every time I saw a small baby there was a gnawing. Finally Del gave me enough money to fly to Arkansas and get the baby. She was eight months old.

Once again circumstances were in our favor. I loved Del but it was a strange kind of love. Underneath it hostility and bitterness began to surface. Though I tried to cover my feelings Del was repulsive to me and I could not stand to have him touch me.

I went back to the University of Washington for more psychiatric treatment. The doctor suggested I get a part-time job as therapy. I went to work as a cocktail waitress. I enjoyed it. I met lots of people. Part time increased to full time. Del was working days and I nights and communications between us were at an all-time low. I hated to come home. Sometimes I stayed out all night and came staggering in at 4:00, 5:00 or 6:00 A.M.

After a few months, when Del could tolerate no more, he gave me a choice. "Either you quit working or I'm leaving you."

I refused to quit.

We let the house go. Del filed for divorce. I sent the children to live with my mother and moved into a small apartment.

With no responsibilities, I was totally free to run. I became involved with a pusher. I was introduced to a new way of life, that of the drug addict. In this new circle of "friends" I met Ed. He told me he had been in jail for child support. I felt sorry for him and let him move in with me. I was to learn much later that he had been booked on suspicion of murder, but was released for lack of evidence. His wife's charred body had been found with her brains beaten out and a stocking tied around her neck.

Ed was temperamental and difficult to live with. He would wake up from a nightmare, screaming and violently frightened. I was afraid of him. Afraid to stay and afraid to leave. He couldn't get a job because of his record and he shot himself full of all kinds of needles. I guess it must have been heroin.

My children came back and I was trying to support them, Ed and my own drug addiction. I got a

15

job in a department store days and danced in a "go-go" place at night, high on drugs most of the time. I took acid, mescaline, speed, anything. I wasn't particular. In a few months I went from a size 14 to a size 6.

One day Ed found a suitcase in the trunk of the car. I had used it when I had taken the children over to Val's, their new foster mother. I had signed a release because I did not feel capable of caring for them any longer.

Ed became hysterical, thinking I was trying to sneak out on him. He took off his shoe and hit me on the head. Again and again and again. Blood was streaming down my face but he kept hitting, harder and harder. "I can't live without you. If you're gonna leave me I'd rather see you dead." He ran upstairs.

I grabbed the car keys off the table and escaped out the front door, blood streaming down my face. Somehow I made it over to Val's and she took me to the hospital. I stayed there two weeks. My head throbbed with pain but the pain in my head was nothing compared to the agonizing pain of withdrawal from drugs in my stomach.

After I was released from the hospital I went to stay with Val and the children. I lived in constant terror, knowing Ed would be looking for me.

I was waiting in the parking lot for Val to come out of a store when I heard a tap on the car window by my head. Startled, I turned. Ed stood there, peering in, his head inches from mine. I started to roll up the car window. He clenched both hands over the top of the window, ripping it out of the car. Pieces of glass shattered to the pavement below.

He flung the car door open, jerked me out and started beating on me. I was stunned and blinded from the blows on my head. He dragged me over to his car, shoved me in, ran around the other side and started the motor. I leaned against the car door, wiggled the handle and it opened. He was hanging on to me with one hand, trying to drive with the other. I jerked free from his grip and tumbled out onto the curb.

A crowd had started to gather and everyone just stood there and stared. Ed pulled a box cutter with a long sharp blade out of his pocket and wiped it on his pants. I heard him say, "The police are going to get me anyway so I might as well kill you."

I kept screaming for help but the people just stood and stared. I looked up and saw Val running down the street towards us. He grabbed my throat. I couldn't breathe. I felt the point of the razor slice into my skin just below my ear. I thought: This is it. It's curtains for you, darlin'.

Val hit him with her fist hard enough to throw him off balance and the razor in his hand slid all the way across my throat to the other earlobe, making a long surface cut. I turned over on my stomach, blood trickling from my neck. I looked up to see him coming at me again with the razor.

Val had lost her balance when she struck him and before she could get to him again he sliced my back open from my neck all the way down to my tailbone. I laid there with my back open and I saw him coming at me again. Val grabbed him. He came down on her with the razor, missing her eye by a fraction of an inch. Blood started spurting out. He stopped, looked at Val and then at me. He dropped the razor, put his hands to his face and began to sob. He ran crying to his car and drove off.

The ambulance came. We were taken to the hospital.

Not one person in that crowd of people would go to court and Ed was still free. Again I lived in fear. A few weeks later, before my back was even healed, I saw him on the street. I was paralyzed, but I was afraid to run from him. He walked up to me and said, "Darlin', I'm sorry." I knew I must have been losing my mind because I still cared for him.

After he cut me up I married him. But it only lasted five months. He started acting strange again. I took my chances, moved into a one-room basement apartment and got another dancing job downtown.

I became more deeply involved with dope addicts and pushers. Drug use was becoming a way of life. I was so high most of the time I didn't know who I was or what I was. I had a lot of "bad trips" and attempted suicide several times.

I took pills to go to sleep. One time I slept for three days without food or water. Every time I woke up I took another sleeping pill.

I bought a gun. I decided if I were going to commit suicide I would blow my brains out.

The social worker asked me to take the children once a week. When they came they always wanted to stay. For the first time in my life I was embarrassed. I wondered how you tell six children their mother can't take care of them because she's hooked on drugs.

One day I turned out all the lights and turned the radio dial until I found some soft music. I wasn't in the mood for rock.

I was lying there half-asleep trying to figure out some way I could straighten out my life.

All of a sudden I heard this "God commercial" on the radio. The voice said, " 'People Who Care' are standing by to talk with you and you can call right now." By the time I found a pencil it was over. I kept listening, hoping I would hear that number again. It came on again and I wrote it down but I didn't have enough courage to call. I started feeling sorry for myself again and thought, "Oh they don't really care, they probably only help white people." But I kept listening to that station every day and after a few days I called.

A girl named Dorothy talked to me. She asked me all about myself. I told her. She said something that amazed me. "God loves you just the way you are. No matter what you've done He accepts you as you are." We talked for quite a while. She really seemed to care. But in the back of my mind was the thought, "Nobody really cares about you, darlin'." And I wondered what the catch was with this "People Who Care" stuff.

In the meantime my children had come for their weekly visit and my oldest son refused to go back to the foster home. I didn't have the heart to send them away.

Dorothy kept calling me to see how I was. I couldn't believe it. Each time we talked she told me more neat stuff about God and Jesus Christ. She made Him seem so real, so touchable.

I had tried everything else. There was not much I hadn't given a try. Why not give God a chance?

I began to believe that God loved me and soon I began to identify with the person of Jesus Christ. Dorothy said that Christ was alive today and He was just waiting to give purpose and meaning to my life. She said He would also provide the power to overcome the problems that were dragging me down and destroying me.

I began to put my trust in God. The changes that took place in my life were gradual but definite. Soon I was able to live without drugs. I had a new source of strength, just like Dorothy had said. I soon learned that I could live one day at a time, facing each day's problems as they came up. I didn't need the crutches I had been using. LSD, speed, mescaline and sleeping pills became a thing of the past. I learned to trust God instead of a pill.

I discovered and am still discovering that trusting God is a gradual process. Like a deep relationship with any friend, it doesn't happen overnight. But as I continue to experience the love of God and His concern for me, I find myself responding to Him and knowing that He has everything under control.

One of the most amazing things that has happened to me is that I have discovered the hatred that I had, especially for whites, has almost disappeared. I used to hate everybody, black and white. I was militant. I never trusted anyone or knew what a friend was. I was out to get whatever I could, however I could get it and I thought everyone else was too.

I have many new friends. People I would have hated before this have become friends I love and trust. Because of the people I have met through the radio station, I have been able to move into a decent home and live a fairly normal life and be a mother to my six children.

My children have become important individuals to me now, where before they were mostly in my way.

There are still many problems that exist and new ones that appear every day. Many of the people I have known in the past have continued to be a part of my life, though in a different way. Before I was one of them. But now that I have a new life, my heart aches to share with them what I have experienced. These people need help so badly.

I have been turned in twice to the Welfare for providing a place for an old friend to stay, but I just can't turn them out on the street.

I have had to use the grocery money to bail a friend out of jail, but I didn't have the heart to just leave him there.

One of my friends who was a prostitute for fifteen years has met Jesus as her friend. She has given up her old life.

Del and I have become good friends and for the first time in my life the bitterness and hatred that I had towards him has disappeared. He comes over to see the children occasionally and is overwhelmed at the change in my life. He keeps thinking it must be time for me to go off the deep end again.

I still have days when I get depressed and occasionally I have a "trip out," a side effect from some "bad trips" I have taken. But I never hit rock bottom or get to the point of taking the escape route through drugs or suicide. I have a Friend who sticks close to me in good times as well as bad and He loves me just the way I am.

3

Three for the Price of One

"Good morning. 'People Who Care.' May we help you?"

Angie gulped. She'd almost phoned this number many times before. Just today she had rummaged around to find a pencil in time to jot it down as it was given over the radio. Now here she was.

"Uh, I'd like to talk to someone about the meaning of life," she said simply.

"Fine," came the friendly voice over the phone. "If I may have your number, I'll have one of our people call you shortly."

As she recited the seven digits on her dial to the faceless voice, she wondered if she had done the right thing in calling. She had no big problem, really—no overwhelming reason to call.

She and Lee had come to Seattle to "get ahead financially." But the change from rural Idaho to the urban world had been more than they had anticipated. Located in a trailer park just off a busy freeway, they were methodically interrupted by the huge jetliners landing and taking off at a nearby municipal airport. Their forty-foot mobile home was sandwiched in between two others just like theirs.

Angie had grown up in the country, living on the ranch her folks had bought when she was just two years old. By the time she was five she was out all day helping her dad with his work around the ranch. Soon she was able to reach the pedals on the "Cat," and her dad taught her to drive the big tractor. He would help her hitch up to a piece of farm machinery and supervise as she and the "Caterpillar" eased it into position. She learned to drop the big blade on the front of the huge machine and soon was able to push logs into piles to be cut up for firewood.

When she started school, Angie found herself surrounded by other children—a new experience for a little girl accustomed to working and playing with adults. Her classmates didn't drive big tractors in the woods; they played games she didn't know. She began to feel different from the others— painfully different—and shy. Whether the kids teased her because she was different from them or because she was an easy target, she didn't know. But school was a difficult and very uncomfortable situation.

When high school graduation was over, Angie

24

went to Spokane to work for the summer. With little experience in managing money, she spent almost all she earned on various trifles, instead of saving for school in the fall.

Autumn came and Angie entered a school of nursing in Spokane. Dormitory life was a very hard adjustment; suddenly having twenty "sisters" was overwhelming to a girl who had never had any close siblings. And Mother wasn't there to take care of her clothes or to make her study every night. At the end of the first semester several girls had to drop out of school because of low grades and Angie was one of them.

She took a job at the hospital as a nurse's aid and moved into an apartment. But managing money was a real problem and living alone became unbearable. After two months Angie went to live with her grandmother. Six months later she reapplied to the school of nursing, and was accepted and granted a second chance.

Still she was fighting the problem of shyness. All through school she had been scared of boys. Several of her friends tried to get her to go out, but their efforts at matchmaking were generally unsuccessful.

Angie noticed the driver of her bus one weekend on the routine bus trip home from school to visit her family. She guessed that he had been on this route for about two or three months, but she had never really seen him before. Lee began a conversation and Angie found herself drawn toward this man who seemed so outgoing, so self-assured, yet genuine. He seemed like an old friend and was easy to talk with. She felt very much at ease with him.

After several weekend trips home, the shy girl felt sure she had found the man she wanted to marry. Lee seemed to really love people and made friends easily, while she remained withdrawn and reserved. He embodied all the things that Angie wanted to be and wasn't.

Her folks failed to share her enthusiasm about Lee. Ten years' difference in their ages seemed to be a real obstacle. And Angie was just finishing her first year of nurse's training. But Angie had her way and they were married just before the following Christmas.

It would have been nice to say the couple lived happily ever after, but such was not the case. Angie discovered that her problems seemed to mushroom rather than diminish. Now, as well as being in the midst of the most difficult part of her nursing education, she also had a house to keep and money to manage. Bills began to accumulate, and Angie toyed with the idea of giving up school and going to work. But Lee's love and encouragement kept her in school and got the bills paid.

Shortly after Angie finished training, Lee's job phased out. They made the decision to come to Seattle. But Seattle was not much better. Both she and Lee yearned for the country. The concrete could not replace the green fields, nor the skyscrapers the trees. Their finances prohibited them from getting away for even a weekend.

The questions began to come. What was life all about? She and Lee would get up in the morning, eat breakfast, go off to work, come home, have dinner, watch TV and go to bed. Day after day. Was there any point to all of this? If so, what was it?

While cleaning the trailer and cooking dinner, Angie started listening to an "easy music" radio station. The format was pleasant after a day's work, and she identified with the sound of a jet as it whooshed across the airways "from Vancouver to Vancouver." Just like home, she thought sardonically.

At first, whenever she would hear one of the "commercials" she would ignore it or deny that to know God would make any difference in her life. But finally she began to listen:

"Friendship means more than acquaintance, kinship, or even love. A friend is someone who's always there . . . good times and bad. It's not so strange then that Christ, talking about how He works in our lives in this twentieth century, says that He's a friend . . . one who's even closer than a brother. And He lives to relate to us in a personal, meaningful way in these difficult days. To know Him as your real Friend, call now. 'People Who Care' are standing by to talk, and they're as near as your phone."

Well, she needed a friend. She and Lee had been in Seattle all this time, and they hadn't made any friends. Funny, she thought, how people can live so close together and be so far apart . . .

Oh, the phone! Well, here goes—

"Hello?"

"Hello, Angie? This is Sue from 'People Who Care,' returning your call."

27

As Angie talked with Sue, she sensed that Sue really did seem to care. So they set up an appointment to meet the following day.

The next day when Sue came to Angie's, both were amazed to discover how much they were alike. Both had grown up in a small rural town and they both had come to the city and gone into nurses' training. And both of them had a real hankering for the country.

The talk drifted toward Angie's reason for calling 'People Who Care.' She told of how the meaninglessness of life had been getting her down, how she felt that there must be more to life than that which she had been experiencing. So Sue related to Angie how she had found the emptiness of her existence filled with peace and purpose when she had been confronted with God Himself.

As Pascal had once said, "Inside every man there is a God-shaped vacuum." And God had filled that terrible void in Sue's life to overflowing with the reality of Himself. Now she found life exciting and positive. "Love is what gives meaning to life," according to Bertrand Russell. Sue had found this to be more than true as she was experiencing God's love for her.

Angie and Sue also talked of how, just as there are laws that govern man's relationship to his physical environment, there are spiritual laws that affect his relationship to God. These laws point out God's love and concern for man and the price He had to pay to reestablish His relationship to man.

Angie understood. She began to see that the loneliness she was experiencing and the disappointment she sensed in her day-to-day life were but symptoms of that God-shaped vacuum that existed in her own heart. So she asked God to fill it.

Gradually, Angie began to feel inwardly a sense of well-being. The circumstances had not changed, but she had. Peace had come to roost in her heart. She began to look beyond the monotony of her daily routine. She and Lee began to formulate plans to move back to Idaho and build a home in the country. Now, in the light of things to come, today had real meaning. Hope replaced despair.

Outwardly, too, Angie changed. She began to feel more at ease in a group of people. She found a new confidence alive within. She even ventured to express her own ideas and found that others readily accepted them and seemed to appreciate her. With Christ's presence, Angie no longer had to "go it alone."

There were also some fringe benefits to her new relationship to Christ, Angie discovered. She and Sue became good friends. Sue didn't seem to be the sober religionist that she might have expected a Christian to be.

One day, the phone rang. "Angie," said Sue, "I know of a gal in your end of town you really should meet. She and her husband have been here for some time and they don't know anyone. Would you give her a call?"

So she took down Debby's number and called. Soon Angie found herself filling a real need for friendship in someone else's life. She and Lee began to see Debby and her husband often. The four of them became good friends. Angie found in the process of meeting Jesus Christ that she made not one new friend but three. That vacuum had not only been filled; it was running over.

Not long ago Angie was asked if all her problems were solved now that she was a Christian.

"No, they aren't," she replied frankly. Then, with a laugh, "But they don't bother me like they used to."

Angie is obviously under New Management.

4

"He Saw the Light"

"I fleshed out again." A pet phrase Scott uses a lot, which to him means he has "lost his cool." Scott has a fascinating story to tell and he delights in telling it. He has found life an exciting adventure since he started walking hand in hand with the One who said, "I have come that you might have life and that you might have it more abundantly."

Scott's life has changed dynamically in the six months he has known Christ. But he isn't perfect yet. He and his wife Brenda, both former drug addicts, have had some serious difficulties adjusting to marriage and to the "straight life." It was after

31

one of their many battles that Scott decided to call
"People Who Care." A promising evening with
friends had ended in disaster. Scott had struck
Brenda, she had fled to the neighbors for comfort
and he sat alone, bewildered. He told the listening
ear on the other end of the line that he loved Brenda but that his ego kept getting in the way. He was
grateful to God for having brought him where he
was; yet, if Christ had anything to do with healing
broken relationships, he wanted to get in on that
too.

Scott and Brenda are young. He is 21 and she 20.
Yet in their short years they have both experienced
a taste of hell on earth.

Scott speaks softly as he relates his trek through
the valley of the shadow. He pauses often, smiles
boyishly, slowly, gently shaking his head, as
though he himself can scarcely believe that much
has happened to him. He is clean-shaven now, his
sandy red hair is trimmed neatly below his ears.
But to him it is short, having lived awhile on the
hippie scene. His conversation is peppered with
such phrases as, "Praise the Lord."

Scott, by his own admission, has always been a
rebel. When he was thirteen he ran away from
home for the first time. Ever since he was very
small he liked to play "war" and thought it would
be exciting to get in on the real thing. At age seventeen he joined the Marines and went to Vietnam. It was during this time he first began to de-
pend on marijuana. It seemed to be a way of life
for many of the boys who found themselves on the
front lines in Vietnam and didn't like being there.

Scott was sent home to recover after being wounded for the second time, only to learn he had orders to go back. That was too much. He had experienced enough bloodshed and real fear in those months that he no longer thought it was exciting to fight in a war. He was convinced in his own mind that he could never go back, at any cost.

He went AWOL.

He started "dropping acid" during his stay in the hospital and rapidly increased his intake after going "over the hill." His first reaction to LSD was ecstatic. He thought, "Wow, the people who invented this stuff really had me in mind."

"It was only a matter of months," Scott said, "before I began to realize that I was no longer using drugs; they were using me. But I kept 'dropping' and running. I had so much acid in my system I was high all the time. I didn't have to 'drop,' I just stayed high. All the people I associated with were drug people. I couldn't even talk to 'straight' people."

After midnight one night Scott and two of his buddies lay gazing into the sky down at Huntington Beach, after having "dropped" three cubes of acid. Through the darkness the sky began to light up, revealing a strange phenomenon. They looked at each other, then back at the sky. They had all three seen it.

To "acid" people, "seeing the light" is supposed to be a sign of having experienced a spiritual rebirth. "Into what I don't know," was Scott's comment in retelling the experience.

They lay on the beach several hours, stoned,

staring into the sky, "rapping" about their experience.

"When we started coming down we saw these funny-looking men dressed in blue uniforms. I was 'over the hill' and plenty scared," Scott recalled. "We were too stoned to walk, but somehow we managed to get to our feet. With the three cops less than five feet behind us, waiting for one of us to drop, we made it up to Main Street and to the Orange County Teen Revival Coffee House. The place was usually packed, but that night there was only one guy there."

Scott talked to the guy in the coffee house for half an hour, relating his experience of having "seen the light."

"I had seen galaxies in the sky and planets revolving around each other. He was polite and listened, but his reaction was, 'So what?' My ego was really hurt. I thought: Man, you don't know who you're talking to. I'VE SEEN THE LIGHT!"

To Scott's amazement he learned that the guy had also "seen the light." He looked at Scott. "Now that you've seen all this, what does it mean to you? How does it all fit together?" Scott hadn't thought of that. He was in no condition to think now, yet the question hit like a bomb. What did it all mean?

"The guy started 'rattling' about Jesus and the meaning of the universe. I was so stoned I 'tubed out' on most of what he was saying. Still my mind seemed clear when he spoke about how God had become a man and entered this universe in spacetime. It began to make a little sense. I didn't remember a lot of what he said, but that night the seeds were planted. It was the beginning of an awareness of the reality of a living God.

"I carried a Bible around for three weeks after that. I don't know why. I didn't read it, it just seemed like a cool thing to do. I didn't know anything about who Jesus was or how to become a Christian. I just knew there was God."

Prior to Scott's experience on the beach, he had become involved with Brenda, also a heavy drug user, and she became pregnant. He returned to Portland to be with her and they decided to get married, if for no other reason, than to reap the military benefits. He was still AWOL, and didn't know what would become of him.

After their marriage they moved to Chicago. It was then Scott decided he had to stop running and turned himself in.

Through a series of miraculous happenings he was given only a small fine, "busted" and given a 30-day suspended sentence after having been "over the hill" 120 days. A few weeks later he was released on a medical discharge—with a pension! "That was one of the happiest days of my life," Scott recalled, grinning.

"Our marriage was a joke," he said. It was just a legal document. We were still 'dropping acid,' still 'turning on,' our lives still centered around drug people. I stopped liking it but I didn't know what to do. I was kind of in a stagnant situation, tired of 'turning on,' but I didn't know what I wanted."

Scott and Brenda could not seem to mesh their lives together. Their marriage was hanging by a thread. They decided a change of scenery would help, so they moved back to Portland, Brenda's hometown.

Scott was becoming painfully aware of the hold drugs had taken on him. He hadn't "turned on" for three months, yet was stoned constantly. When he made it known to his "friends" that he no longer wanted to "turn on," they rejected him. Drugs seemed to be the thing that held users together. Most of Scott's and Brenda's companions were "hooked" and a lot of them had progressed to "shooting smack" (heroin). Scott wanted no part of it but Brenda had passed the point of no return.

Nearly a year had passed since Scott's experience at Huntington Beach. The seeds that were planted there at the Orange County Teen Revival Coffee House had never completely left Scott's subconscious. It became more and more evident to him that there must be something to what he had heard about Jesus, but he didn't know what to do with it.

On a Friday evening, after Scott and Brenda had been arguing all week, they decided to call it quits. Scott packed a small seabag and boarded a bus—to where he didn't know. On the bus his mind was in a turmoil. Nothing seemed to make sense or have any real purpose. He got off at a park where a lot of "hippie" people were gathered. He bought some LSD, took it and sat down on a park bench.

That was the first time Scott had "turned on" in quite a few months. "It was something else," he said. "My mind was spinning. I was stoned and I felt 'superlost.' My mind kept asking questions like, 'What am I gonna do?' And back would come an answer, an internal voice, 'What can you do?' I looked around at the people in the park and thought to myself, 'This park is an evil place. The park isn't so bad, it's the people in it.' Then it came to me again. That voice. 'You are just the same as the rest of the people in the park, doing the same thing they are.' I walked up a winding trail through some trees and the voice came to me again. This time it was, 'I am holding you together.' I knew it wasn't the drugs. I looked around at the trees and all the things that were really neat and I realized what a joke I was doing. I think I even yelled out loud, 'You're right.' "

Scott knew he had to find the personality behind that voice.

He sat down on a bench next to a small group, playing guitars. The music sounded good and Scott thought these people were the only decent people in the park. He stared at them for several minutes, becoming totally enmeshed in the sweetness of their music. They got up and left and two more people sat down and "shot up some smack." The sight sickened him and he ran out of the park after the others. He talked to them for a while, then they took him to a place called "Rap-line." It was good to have someone to talk to but they weren't able to help him.

He hitched a ride across town. He wanted to see Brenda. He had hopes that they could work out their problems. When he arrived Brenda was just leaving, and she wasn't interested in talking to Scott.

All his hopes were shattered now. His plans were shot down and he didn't know where to turn. "I guess I must have sat on the curb for 45 minutes," Scott recalled. "I went to a phone booth and called the 'Rap-line' people again. They said, 'We can't tell you what to do.' I called some other people I knew. Nobody had any answers.

I stepped out of the phone booth and thought I'd go see some friends. They were drug people, but I had to talk to someone.

At the same moment the voice came to me again. 'Go to the church on the corner.' I had been there twice with Brenda. We had gone to make each other happy. I had met the minister and liked him. He had been an alcoholic and had lost his family almost the same way I had. I thought he might have some answers.

"I was superstoned and could barely put one foot in front of the other, yet I ran the three blocks to the church."

The minister remembered Scott and told him he had just been thinking about him. He offered his hand, but Scott said, "Look, I don't have time to shake hands or be friendly. I'm in trouble and I need help."

Scott poured out his story, then asked in bewilderment, "What am I going to do?" He felt he had to make some kind of decision. The thought of suicide entered his mind. After all, what had he to live for? Unless—unless he could start all over.

As they talked, the truth began to unfold to him that with Christ he could start over. He learned that Christ was in the business of rebuilding lives. He would not only forgive Scott's past and wipe the slate clean, but He would throw away the slate.

That sounded cool to Scott, so right then and there he knelt and prayed. He said, "I expected an explosion or something, but nothing happened." He concluded that Jesus Christ didn't want anything to do with him.

"I was still stoned and very psychedelic," he said, "and this great big word D-O-U-B-T spelled out across my mind. I knew that doubt was the only thing that kept me from believing. The doubt left and I knew that Jesus Christ had entered my life. I had a feeling of deep peace mingled with joy and excitement—and I was sober! I was jumping around there like a jackrabbit and I must have shaken hands with the minister twelve times."

Scott spent the next three days at a place called Shiloh, a Christian commune, where he met others who had gone through similar experiences in the drug scene. It was a great time of becoming acquainted with the personality who had invaded his life. "For the first time in my life I knew I was really living," Scott said.

Strangely enough Shiloh was only a few blocks from where Brenda lived. He let her know what had happened to him and where he would be in case she needed him. Later that week he and one of his new friends spent a few days on a huge piece of land near Eugene owned by the people who owned Shiloh. They enjoyed the seclusion. They just wanted to get to know Christ better.

Scott's great joy was mingled with sadness as he thought of Brenda. He wanted her to know Christ too. He returned to Portland.

Brenda had gone deeper into drug dependency

and was starting to turn to hard drugs. A warrant was out for her arrest and she had been kicked out of her apartment. When Scott returned to Portland he found her at Shiloh. That night, exactly one week after Scott had met Jesus Christ, his prayers were answered and Brenda too trusted Christ.

Scott and Brenda stayed at Shiloh for two months. Brenda didn't need to take acid, speed, or smack anymore. She was really "turned on" now and she was depending on God for her "kicks."

They moved to Seattle and Scott found a job there.

When Scott called "People Who Care," he and Brenda were again having serious conflicts. He was right in presupposing that God could relate to this problem; after all He had already brought them through a heap of troubles.

As "People Who Care" have marveled time after time, the calls always seem to be channeled to the right person. Scott and Brenda's problem was not unusual. Conflict in marriage seems to be the norm, even among Christian couples. Jerry, the one who returned Scott's call, was able to share from his own experience some valuable things that God had revealed to him just a short time ago after seventeen years of a stalemate relationship.

Jerry and his wife spent time with Scott and Brenda on several occasions, sharing things from their own lives.

After a few weeks Jerry called back to see how Scott and Brenda were doing. Scott said, "Man, I don't know what's happened, but I really feel different towards Brenda. I don't lose my cool so much and I'm beginning to enjoy just being with her." Brenda smiled, "We are just like newlyweds."

Scott and Brenda's problems are not all solved. They have been through a lot of "fleshy" things, as Scott would say, but they have both "seen the Light" now—the real Light, the Light of the world—and they didn't find it in a cube of LSD.

5

"Free Indeed"

Ever since Eleanor can remember, her subconscious mind has been haunted by the underlying awareness that somewhere there is a God and that somehow she must find Him.

Eleanor is a typical American housewife. Her life-style resembles that which you would expect to find in suburbia. Her roles include wife, mother, chauffeur, nurse, church member and coffee clatcher.

To add variety to the routine of her daily life, she had taken a few classes, dabbled a little in the arts, but had found nothing to fill what seemed to be a vacancy in her life.

She found a challenging job with a real estate firm. It provided an outlet, but also a temptation to stay out late at night and have a couple drinks with the other girls in the office. It wasn't long before she decided it would be wise to quit.

The tendency to sip a few drinks occasionally in the evening was an easy pattern to fall into. It was one of those evenings when Eleanor had felt particularly melancholy and was flipping the radio dial, that she was stimulated by a voice that said in essence, "You could know God." A telephone number was given and the voice on the radio was inviting her to call.

Find God? She thought. She jotted down the number. She had had just enough to drink to give her the courage she needed to dial the number.

Eleanor thought of the many books she had read about religion. She had studied all the great religions of the world, while still remaining an active church member, but had not come up with an answer that could satisfy the churning in her life.

Religion, she had always thought in the back of her mind, should be simple. Yet everything she had heard or read was complicated.

She placed the call and found herself talking to a girl named Jill. "Not wanting to appear ignorant," she said, "I merely told Jill I was curious about 'People Who Care.' She told me their function was to help people who were interested in finding a meaningful relationship with God. That was what I wanted."

Jill and Eleanor talked awhile about a lot of things, then Jill suggested they get together with another friend for coffee.

Eleanor was amazed when she met Jill and her

friend. "They both seemed to emit a quiet confidence, yet an overwhelming sense of exuberance. Freedom! That was it!" she exclaimed. "They had freedom and I didn't. I remembered a Bible verse I had once heard but had never understood. It was 'If the truth shall make you free, you shall be free indeed.' I wondered now if I was seeing the kind of freedom the Bible spoke of."

As the three women talked, Eleanor heard things she had not heard anywhere before. Simple things. She heard that God loved her with a kind of love that does not seek anything in return or demand a response. She heard that Christ had paved the way back to God for every person since Adam. That his death on the cross had provided total permanent forgiveness and eternal life for anyone who was willing to accept a free gift, with no strings attached.

It was all too simple, she thought. A simple answer was what she had always wanted.

That morning Eleanor responded to God's love. "I had always wanted to have Christ in my life," she said. "I had been through the church routine. Baptism, confirmation, church membership. The works. I knew down inside that I wasn't where I wanted to be, but I didn't know how to get there.

"As I tried to follow a certain religious code, I was left with the impression that religion had to be tied in a neat little package. The problem was, I couldn't keep the package together. I could not measure up to the standards in the New Testament that I thought a Christian should."

Experiencing what she had heard was a long

uphill climb for Eleanor. Although she met weekly with other Christians and learned more and more about the Person she had responded to, she was pulled in different directions for many months.

Her religious background was a hindrance to a spontaneous relationship with God. She had been taught that God expected her to behave a certain way, which she had tried to do. She was often convinced that she must be on a performance basis in order to please God.

She was continually haunted by the thought that Jill and her friends might be heretics. She had read in the Bible that there would be false prophets. She was reluctant to put her trust in their words, yet she was intrigued and drawn to them as a result of their carefree life-style and their apparent love for one another and for her.

"The turmoil in my life continued for about nine months," Eleanor said. "One day I received a book in the mail from 'People Who Care.' It was called 'Love Is Now.' It had a bright pink and purple psychedelic cover and looked interesting enough to open immediately.

"As I read, the truths that Jill and her friends had been drilling into me all those months began to unfold. The idea of heresy dropped like scales from my eyes as I began to experience in my own life the forgiveness and freedom that I had seen in theirs."

There was no room to doubt whether these things were true any longer. Eleanor was now experiencing firsthand the freedom that she had been searching for all of her life.

Eleanor very soon came to realize that God wasn't expecting her to measure up to the New Testament standard, which would be perfection, but that He loved her just as she was.

"This set me free to be myself," she said. "And to be satisfied with myself. Soon I was able to accept others just as they were, realizing that perfection was not the criterion for gaining God's favor, but that it was simply trusting in what Christ had already accomplished over 2,000 years ago.

"One of the neatest things I discovered just recently," Eleanor said with excitement, "is that I don't have to make excuses anymore for my bad behavior. Knowing that God forgives me, it sets me free to forgive myself."

Eleanor's long search for a simple answer has ended. Though the answer was simple, the benefits are compound and at last she is "Free Indeed."

6

Where the Grass Is Greener

Deana strode down the hall, books under her arm. She flipped her auburn hair back over her shoulder; now it was long enough to do that. A wild geometric print shirt topped the new corduroy miniskirt she had just hemmed up last night. Six months ago, twenty pounds ago, she would have looked hideous in such an outfit. She waved to Nick.

High school was a gas.

So was Nick. She sat two seats away from him in geometry class and they had hit it off right away. It was so neat going with someone you could look up to. Nick was six foot four.

Maybe she was growing up. She and her mom had really had some good talks together lately. They were beginning to understand each other finally. Last year she had been so impatient with her folks. They just didn't understand. And she had been disillusioned to find out that parents were just people; she could no longer put them on a pedestal. But all that was okay. She had Someone Else on that pedestal now.

Junior high had really been a drag. Deana and her family had moved here from California during her last year of grade school. They had bought a large older home in the suburbs and set out to give it a much-needed face-lifting.

Deana liked the pseudocountry, all right. Walking to the school bus stop in early autumn, she would watch the sun sift down through the red and yellow leaves marking an erratic path of brightness down the dew-damp road. The winter was beautiful, too. Going outside to hear the hush of snow fall from the gray sky to indiscriminantly blanket the slender branches of denuded trees, fence post tops, fields and roofs gave you the feeling of being the only person in the world. And spring, silently sneaking up on you, surprising you with its first touch of new green or an unexpected gray pussy willow, gave you the delightful sense of intruding on Nature.

Remodeling the house had been lots of fun. Coming home from school, Deana looked forward to the sweet smell of sawdust from a newly cut beam or the sharp odor of freshly stained panelling. In the evenings at dinner the family would talk over what had been accomplished and what was yet to be done—what color would be best for the hall carpet, and where should the kitchen counter go. This was their home.

And then it was finished. Two and one-half years of work and plans had resulted in a spacious two-story home surrounded by an expansive cedar deck. The lovely greenhouse stood overlooking the road, a monument to what can be accomplished by a family working together.

Deana had expected that now since the house was finished, her folks would argue less. The color of the new bathroom that had caused such dissension had long ago been slapped on the wall. That new-type kitchen tile that was the result of a stalemate instead of an agreement was now on the floor.

Now her folks argued about other things—things much more vague, things Deana didn't understand. Sometimes she would think her mom was the good guy; other times, her dad. It sure was hard to tell who wore the white hat when.

And then last year came the divorce. Dad had moved out leaving Deana and her mom to work out their own hassles. The two of them seemed never to agree on anything. That's when she had picked up grass. Marijuana was easy to come by and her friend, Susy, always wanted a piece of the action. Getting high together gave them both a sense of belonging and an escape from the here-and-now.

Grass was where it was at. The girls had found a baby-sitting job that paid off well—in marijuana.

After their charges were tucked in for the night, Susy and Deana would spend the remainder of the evening smoking up their earnings.

"Come fly with me in my beautiful balloon." Pot was the most. Getting off the ground was a little tough the first time Deana lit a joint; but after five minutes or so, the dizziness yielded to a floating weightlessness that lifted you up, up, up, and away from the hassles that closed in on you.

Reality was there—really there: Getting high just laid you back—stripped off all the external tension —and you began to slow down to see things, think about things, that had never hit you before. Everything came into sharper focus. The print on the newspaper stood out in bold relief; the design in the tapestry possessed a third dimension. The ordinary became extraordinarily vivid. Turn up the stereo. Echo . . . echo . . . echo . . . the sound hollows out and mellows into softness. You're walking the beach in your mind, inundated by the splash, splash, splash of waves. Wah, wah, wah; the music sweeps up over the surf, taking you with it. Groove with the vibrations. Lay back . . . sink into smoothness. Fill your head with the sound, sound, sound, sound . . . Sleep. Sleep. Sleep.

But what goes up must come down. When cold-water reality splashes in your face after you come back, you face your life-style for what it really is: sloppy clothes, hanging with the crowd, skipping school and a grade point plummeting straight to zilch. The price of belonging.

Then, of course, there was God. Deana thought a lot about Him. What if He should come when she was stoned? Maybe finding Him was the answer. But where to look? All she had ever heard of God and heaven sounded beautiful. And yet the discrepancy of real life told her that it all was so very far away.

Deana toyed with the idea of suicide. Dad had all sorts of electronic gadgets in the basement. She had spent hours down there looking over the stuff; touch the right spot and it's all over, baby. Certainly God was beyond death. But she couldn't be quite sure enough to trip out. Supposing she were wrong? Suicide would eliminate all further possibilities of search.

It was late summer after a come-down that she called "People Who Care." She and Mom had had another row late that night, and she had retreated to her room to flick on the radio and lose herself and her problems in sound.

"Nobody cares. Nobody cares!" she sobbed as she buried her head in the pillow.

But that isn't what she heard over the radio:

" 'People Who Care' are standing by to talk with you. They're as near as your phone."

"I've got to check this out," she murmured as she began to dial.

Fred was on at the station that night. He had been at the "Q" for just a few months and filled in as the night announcer reporting the weather and news as well as relaying calls for "People Who Care."

When Line 4 rang, he automatically checked the roster to see who was on that night and picked up the receiver.

"What is this 'People Who Care' bit all about?" demanded Deana's voice.

They talked for some time and Deana heard that people care because God cares, that God cared for her. It all sounded so logical. This guy, Fred. He was proof. Didn't he care enough to listen to a total stranger?

Knowing someone cared made it easy to "let it all hang out." Deana found herself unloading to Fred; telling him all the ugly things she'd been feeling. All the uncertainties she wrestled with didn't seem to make any difference to him. She could not shock him. He countered all Deana's "confessions" with a response of love and concern.

Deana called Fred several times after that when she was uptight. One night though, he wasn't on; Deana was put through to Lois. Lois told her the same thing—God loves you, God cares.

Intellectually, Deana came to believe that God really did love her. She became so convinced that she turned her life over to Him. She and Lois got together a few times and they became good friends. But there was still a credibility gap between what Deana knew about God and what she experienced.

Deana spent a week at Keystone later that summer. Kathy, her sister's friend, brought over a brochure about the camp and the girls pored over it with interest. It sounded cool—horses, swimming, boys. What a scene for a vacation!

Keystone was everything Deana had anticipated and more. The chapel services and the evening firesides were more than church-as-usual—they were directions that Deana could follow as she searched for God as reality. They sang the neatest songs, songs that assured Deana that God is alive and well.

Bob, the camp director, didn't talk about the sweet bye-and-bye; he told it like it is. God is now, he said. God takes the initiative, you can respond. He doesn't demand, "You do your part, I'll do mine." He does it all.

"Okay, God, I want you to do it for me. Prove to me You're real, and that You love me," Deana whispered to Him one night in chapel.

Suddenly, pow! She knew. She knew. Happiness and certainty rushed over her, carrying her along in the warmth of new security. She wanted to stand up and shout.

"I've got it! I've got it!" she repeated over and over to herself. "I've got Him!"

That week at Keystone had changed her. Rather, God had changed her. She knew He loved her now; she was experiencing it. He was always there, and she knew she could count on Him. Like having a boy friend, but better.

Love changes things. Her folks noticed it. Here was Deana, who had previously demanded understanding, taking time and effort to understand them.

What had happened? Deana, whose radio blared all night because she couldn't go to sleep with all that quiet. Now she drifted off to sleep to the sound of silence.

What had happened? Deana, who slept with the light on because she was afraid of the dark, who stuffed two pillows between her bed and the wall because you couldn't be sure what might lurk in the dark under your bed, who always slept with her feet covered for fear that something might grab her toes. Now she didn't need the light anymore, or the extra pillows.

It would be wrong to leave the impression that, since Deana and God became good friends, she lived happily ever after. There are still tiffs at home as Deana and her mother try to reconcile their viewpoints. There are times she still experiences the sharp pang of growing pains.

But underneath it all, there is that crazy peace—peace you can't explain and you can't understand. Peace you can just enjoy.

Patience, security, love. And peace. This is her new life-style. And what a way to fly!

7

Wait Till Morning

Two months after the accident Dennis came out of the coma.

He lay there a long time, thinking, trying to recall something, anything. It was as though a thick black fog had shrouded his senses. He tried sitting up. Weakness pulled him back down. After a few more attempts he was finally able to sit up. He pulled back the bedcovers and one by one pulled his feet out.

He sat on the edge of the bed dangling his feet on the cold bare floor. The room seemed to have a strange familiarity. Perhaps it was an odor. Something seemed familiar, yet everything was so very strange.

Dennis rubbed his eyes. He was awake. He was quite sure of that. But where was he? Who was he? When he was finally able to open his eyes he surmised that it must be the middle of the night.

Slowly he pushed himself up to a standing position. Still leaning heavily against the bed, he stood in the cold darkness for what seemed like forever.

Deliberately, cautiously, he began to put one foot in front of the other. He carefully felt his way along the rough stucco wall until he reached what felt like a door. He fumbled, then found a doorknob and turned it. The door squeaked as it opened. Dazed and weak, his thin legs shaking under him, Dennis stood.

Slowly he turned his head around the quiet room. He touched his bearded face with surprise. Two dark shadows seemed to be moving around the room.

"How does it feel to be blind, Dennis?" Dennis? Dennis who? Who am I? Oh, yes, Dennis. Dennis Sutton. But where am I? That voice. My brother. My brother, Dan. That's his voice. But what does he mean, blind? I'm not blind, it's just night.

His family had been forewarned by the doctor that when Dennis awoke from the coma he would be without sight. In spite of the preparation, it was an awkward predicament for his brother and mother.

The smaller of the two figures moved across the room towards him. He flinched, then felt a soft warm hand touch his arm. He recognized his mother's voice. "Sit down over here Dennis," she said softly. She led him by the arm to the old flowered overstuffed chair. He turned and felt the familiar shape of the arm, the back, the seat. He sunk down into the chair, exhausted, dazed and bewildered. He leaned his head back on the soft cushions. Remembering.

Dennis had gone with Beth for over a year. He was pretty stuck on her. They had had their differences and called it quits more than once, but somehow they always seemed to end up together again. Beth meant a lot to Dennis. He needed her a lot more than he cared to admit to himself.

Dennis had anticipated with pleasure their date that evening. When Beth called and cancelled for no apparent reason, she was very cold and impersonal. Dennis was hurt and angry. He dressed anyway and drove down to one of his favorite hangouts. He ordered a pitcher of beer, sat down at a small round table alone and unconsciously drank the whole thing. He stared ahead through the squirming topless go-go dancers.

Eventually bored with the half-naked women, he spotted an old buddy. After a lot of back slapping and handshaking, they got into a friendly two-dollar game of pool.

Dennis was a good pool player. Not a hustler, but darn good. Between shots he "chugalugged" a few more beers. Gradually the disappointment of the evening began to wear off, and he thought to himself, "Well, maybe she did have a good reason."

When Beth bounded through the swinging bar doors and shouted his name, Dennis was stunned. She jumped up on a tabletop and began shouting obscenities. She called Dennis every dirty name she could think of and added a few he had never heard. She turned on her heel and disappeared as suddenly as she had entered.

Dennis returned to the pool table and picked up the cue. He leaned far over the large green oblong table, deliberately, carefully lining up his shot. Pretending to ignore the churning that was going on inside, he closed one blurry eye and shot. The eight ball dropped into the pocket.

Dennis reached for his wallet, which contained $128. It was gone.

His face turned white. His hand was shaking as he poured the last few drops of beer from the large glass pitcher. "Down the hatch," he laughed hysterically, half-staggering and half-running out into the street.

His head was twirling, spinning, as he drove his yellow Mustang into the black night. He screeched out of the parking spot and pulled up to a stoplight.

The engine roared in neutral, Dennis' foot heavy on the gas pedal. When he was sure as he could be that all was clear, he shifted and stepped on the gas. The car swerved around the corner in a right turn into six lanes of oncoming traffic.

"I remember going through a tunnel," Dennis recalled. "When I came out of the tunnel, I saw a lot of headlights coming towards me. Four, six, eight pairs. I jerked the wheel to the right and looked down at the speedometer. At eighty-five miles an hour the car left the road. The last thing I remember I was flying through the air. I was told my head had smashed into a tree."

It was difficult and confusing for Dennis to face the cold, dark fact that never again would he drive a car, see a July sunset, or look into the eyes of his girl. All the things pertaining to sight that had always been taken for granted began to haunt him. He realized he would never be independent, never be able to go anywhere alone and never see anything but dark shadows and thousands and thousands of tiny flashing lights dancing, dancing in front of his eyes, almost as though in mockery.

Dennis has spent countless hours, days and months in seclusion, grappling with the stark reality of his blindness. He has searched for help from an endless list of ministers, social workers and various counselors. He has asked himself and others a thousand times, "Why?"

Why, why, why? Is this God's way of punishing me for one bad mistake? If there is a God. If there is a hell I must be in it now. What kind of a loving God would make people suffer? It would be better to be dead, he thought.

Daytime, nighttime, morning, evening. They were all the same to Dennis. All blended together into one endless, meaningless string.

That is perhaps why it was 4:30 A.M. when he called "People Who Care." He sat alone waiting to die. He had turned on all the gas outlets in his dingy basement hotel room, then waited.

What thoughts go through a person's mind as he contemplates death face-to-face? Is there life after death? Is there really a God? How will He punish me for this? What is hell like? I wonder what my mother will think. Well, she couldn't help me. No one could. I wonder if Beth will miss me. Will she be sorry? She'll be sorry. Nobody will ever miss me. I'll probably lay up here and rot. What will happen to my stereo and TV? I wonder if Jesus is really alive.

He waited there in the dingy fume-filled room for death, his only friend, to release him and swallow him up. Then he recalled a number he had recently heard on the radio. The number followed a short quip about a God who cared and understood. The soothing voice on the radio had said something about "People Who Care." Was there really someone who cared about me, Dennis wondered to himself. Surely there wasn't, he answered his own question.

He waited awhile longer, then dialed the time. The melancholy-sounding voice on the other end of the line said, "The tiyem is noww fower-tweentee-fiyive."

He felt somewhat disappointed and somewhat relieved that he was not yet dead. What had gone wrong? It shouldn't take that long to die.

He dialed the "People Who Care" number. The night announcer put him in touch with Jerry, one of the "People Who Care." Jerry and Dennis talked a long time. Dennis heard things that sounded new and even a little promising to him.

For the first time in three and a half years Dennis began to have some positive thoughts. Maybe there really is some hope for me. I guess I'm not the only person in the world who can't see. Some people don't have legs. And some people have to stay in bed for the rest of their lives. At least I can walk around.

Maybe God really does care about me. I wonder if I would have given God a second thought if this hadn't happened. If I had gone through my whole life being able to see, I would never have needed God. And eternity is a long time to spend in hell compared to maybe fifty or sixty years of being blind here on earth. I suppose I could even learn braille.

As the conversation continued into the dawning of a new day, Dennis excused himself from the telephone, walked through the fume-enveloped room and turned off the gas. He opened a small smoke-stained window as far as it would go and returned to the phone.

They have spent a lot of time together, Dennis and Jerry. Dennis is still grappling for the answers to many questions. He is quite sure that God has touched his life in a real way, though he has not found the peace that he is still seeking. He is uncertain about his eternal destiny and not sure of his worth as a member of the human race. His confidence is increasing little by little as he is continually reminded that there really are "People Who Care."

Dennis thinks "People Who Care" are all right. Anyway they saved his life, even though he has times when he wishes they hadn't.

Jerry took Dennis to dinner one night not long ago. As they walked slowly up the crooked wooden stairs of his mother's old house, Dennis stroked his black beard and turned to Jerry. "You're just not like anyone I've ever met. I don't understand you. Why should you do all this just for me?"

8

Beyond the Blue Horizon

"Are you a Christian, Bobbie?" I had never been asked such a pointed question about anything so personal, and it echoed over and over in my mind. How absurd I thought. I'm not a Buddhist, a Hindu or a Moslem, so I must be a Christian. Yet, now that the question had been asked, I wasn't so sure.

I had dialed the "People Who Care" number one morning after hearing a catchy spot about patience. I had been listening to KBIQ for nearly a year now, since I discovered it on the dial, and considered the station an old friend.

When Tricia suggested getting together for coffee I was a bit reticent, being somewhat shy of new people. But I decided I had nothing to lose, really.

I had pictured in my mind's eye a matronly, missionary type, and was astonished when a young-looking "with it" girl drove up in a shiny red sports car. And even more astounded when that girl began to talk about Jesus Christ as though He were a personal friend; even more, her reality and life. She was radiant with a supernatural joy and I was intrigued. I immediately felt as though I were renewing an old friendship rather than meeting a stranger.

Her thoughts on church were like a breath of fresh air. I had tried the church with all of its sacraments, rituals and perfect-attendance buttons, only to end up at age 43 empty. I knew church attendance had little to do with what I was seeking.

I was an "army brat," nurtured on structure and performance. Even a small girl's playtime was within the framework of an army post and it's regulations.

I was baptized by the chief of chaplains, which according to my mother's demeanor, seemed to grant me some sort of dispensation.

My Sunday School years are a blur of black patent leather "Mary Janes," shiny with vaseline, white sox, white cotton gloves and a dime tied tightly in the corner of a white linen hanky.

I sang "Jesus Loves Me" and received a Bible for perfect attendance, but God was not down where I lived. I said my prayers every night: "Now I lay me down to sleep. . . ." But God was not a reality in my life.

In my early teens I went to many churches. Perhaps the inner man was becoming hungry. I tried them all: Baptist, Presbyterian, Episcopal, Jewish and Catholic, but nothing real ever happened. I experienced a subtle restlessness, but no real relationship with God. I had everything I needed materially—loving parents, a good life in a big city, plenty to eat and wear. I even had a taste of civilians and to my surprise they turned out to be real live people.

The war came. I saw my father go from captain to full colonel in three and a half years. From a relaxed civilian life, back to being a real soldier, and then finally to war in Europe. I rather enjoyed the drama of having my father fighting. I don't think I ever really believed for a minute Dad wouldn't come home. I went to church with Mother, but I never asked God to take care of Dad. Mother must have, I thought, because he came home safe and sound.

I met and almost fell in love with a cadet at West Point. I quickly ended the relationship when I learned he was Jewish. I could not accept the prospect of living the rest of my life with a man who didn't believe Jesus Christ was the Son of God. Christ wasn't a reality in my own life, but the whole idea just didn't fit the frame.

Life whirled around me. College weekends at West Point were all very glamorous, yet so very empty.

Then it all changed. I did not and could not know how much, but all the way from Washington D. C. to Fort Lewis the song, "Beyond the Blue Horizon", kept running through my mind.

Within three months I had met and fallen in love with a civilian. Dad had orders to go to Germany and the thought of more structured army life and more moving repulsed me.

I was married at Fort Lewis, but not until my mother's wish was granted. I was confirmed in the Episcopal church. It satisfied my mother, but how could it satisfy me when it wasn't my hunger that was being appeased?

Children appeared in somewhat staggered proggression. A gnawing hunger began to manifest itself, only it showed more on the scales in the bathroom than anywhere else. I wandered in and out of shops, buying things and always still searching—for what I had no idea. But there was a vast vacuum screaming to be filled. I tried to fill it over and over with food and doodads. The hunger grew and physically so did I.

I attended church sporadically with the children but it seemed so phony, so meaningless and so unrealistic. God seemed more dead in church than anywhere else. I thought something must be wrong with me. Everyone else seemed to think it was all right.

Jean moved next door. She and I became close friends. We knew each other so well that it was like two screaming, hungry hearts crying out together. No one ever had more fun being miserable together, though I'm sure at that time neither of us knew how miserable.

I moved. My problems increased. My husband lost his job and we had just had our third child. During the entire ten months I felt as though I were in mourning. I wanted desperately for someone to take it away—the hunger, the thirst, the emptiness. My father helped. My father-in-law helped, but I guess I was really looking for my "Father."

I was given a book called *God Is the Answer,* and there I began to see the shadow of what I wanted. I felt as though perhaps I could have permission to stop worrying, yet it didn't seem human not to worry when your husband is out of work.

Well, Bob did find a job and soon we settled back down to the nine-to-five routine and God was still not a reality in my life, though I thought He might have had something to do with that job.

I was thankful for the new "rut," but it wasn't long before I sensed the presence of that vacuum again, and the scales in the bathroom rose higher and higher.

I tried so hard to be happy but I felt I was playing a role and fooling no one. I went to church but never heard that I was all right or that I was loved. I missed my parents and felt rejected by them, since they seldom communicated with me. I was so hungry, so lonely and so scared. I asked for help from relatives but only got censure. I guess they thought I wanted pity. I was only screaming for acceptance, for love, for a relationship no human can give to another.

The darkness grew, a cold unfriendly darkness with the illness of my husband. It was his heart. He was so terrified he would die it paralyzed his entire being. Little by little he gave up more and more. He was dying inch by inch, in the most agonizing way a man can almost die. He went to work but came home early almost every day.

As money problems increased, my anxiety towered. Despair became a way of life. Tearful prayers poured from my lips but nothing happened. I felt so alone.

I thought of the possibility that I was being tested. I asked to be either passed or flunked. The more I struggled the deeper I sank, and of course, the deeper my husband sank.

Then another ray of light. A hypnotherapist was recommended. I found some peace in his words which were the words of Jesus: "I will never leave you nor forsake you." I saw a momentary pinprick of light, but it quickly went out again as I tried to master the technique of self-hypnosis.

Again striving and straining, I slipped back into the mire of compulsive eating. My husband's chest pains increased and my terror changed to profound apathy. The small sip of water had not quenched the thirst, but only increased it until it seemed as though it could never be satisfied.

Finally I got mad! Real mad! But of course, as female-type mortal wives will, I got mad at my husband and asked him if he were testing me to see how much I would take before I left him. I was all prepared, armed with vindictiveness, to scream "I've had it, I'm leaving now"—when what rolled out instead, in a waterfall of words—"There is nothing you can do that will make me leave you." I looked over my shoulder to see who said that.

When I next talked to his doctor, instead of tattling, I asked how I might help my husband help himself.

That was April 1, 1969, and he hasn't been to the

doctor with chest pains since. I was thrilled and awed. In view of what had happened I thanked the doctor profoundly, and also mumbled an automatic, "Thank God," as crisis Christians often do.

In the summer the Boeing layoffs began and Bob's turn came in July. The last week he was at Boeing, I began putting my hand out to God. I read, reread, almost assimilated my book, *God Is the Answer*. I felt as though my heart and my mind, my faith and my reason were all in mortal combat. But faith became a little stronger and I pretended not to be afraid. My constant liturgy was "God is, God can, God will, God does." Bob got a job, in fact never missed a day, and we both thanked God amidst hugs and kisses.

Just before I had lost contact with my once-close friend Jean, she had been having her own set of problems. She had contemplated and even attempted suicide, divorce and many of the avenues humans try when in despair. Our visits had finally dwindled to nothing, and for six years I neither heard of nor from her. I sent cards at Christmas but never stopped by or called. In a sense I was afraid to since my own darkness didn't contain enough light to help myself, much less someone in the kind of straits Jean had been in.

Through circumstances Jean and I were to meet again. I was overwhelmed to discover that Jean was no longer in despair. There was no depression, no anxiety. She had a light, a radiance and a genuine joy. Not the hysteria of the earlier years.

Our visits increased. My interest in what Jean had to say increased. After thousands of dollars spent on doctors, medicine and psychiatrists—after all those years of searching, Jean had found a peace that could not be shaken. She had obviously come out of her darkness and despair into light and joy.

What was that she had said, I wondered to myself. Born again?

Jean took hold of my hand as we parted one day, and I grasped hers. Off I went with a new ray of hope.

Jean gave me a lot of books. She wanted to give me her light, her joy, her peace.

I read Edgar Cayce, Dr. Ernest Holmes, Robert Frost's *Aglow with the Spirit,* and many others. I acquired all the knowledge I could about God, Jesus, and the spirit world but was still not aware of God being a reality in my life. I knew nothing of a personal relationship with Jesus, though I sure hoped He had a basket full of goodies in store for me.

I was thrilled for a time over the fact that I didn't have to worry so much, so hard. God would take care of everything I thought. But our financial picture began to worsen and the struggle outward and inward started again and panic settled on me.

I wanted so desperately to be out from under the financial pile. I prayed and prayed again. Did you hear me Lord? Did I say it right? Then I began to worry, not so much that God didn't hear me, but that He would say no. I kept looking over my shoulder, wanting to be assured that money would come in to pay the bills. Just when confidence would well up I would think: How can I be so sure

—am I able to second-guess God? My life was a mishmash of doubt, fear, impatience with my husband, my children and everything I touched.

I tried positive thinking. It seemed to work for a while, then fear, more bills, less patience. . . .

Then there was that spot on the radio about patience and the phone call and meeting Tricia, and that all-consuming question, "Are you a Christian, Bobbie?"

Through our meeting I was introduced to a whole new concept of Christianity. I was intrigued because Tricia not only knew Jesus Christ as her personal friend, but she even identified with Peter and Paul and others who seemed to have had some of the same problems people have today. She was so real, so confident and relaxed.

Tricia shared a lot with me about my standing with God. She told me that God loved and accepted me just as I was and that there was nothing I could do to please Him since He was already pleased in His Son. Not a lot sank in, though I was trying very hard to believe it. I did feel a little closer to God, so much closer that when Christmas rolled around that year it didn't seem quite so phony. Oh, there was still tinsel and glitter as before but I was more aware of whose birthday it was.

With the death of Bob's mother came the matter of her estate. One-fifth of it was to be Bob's. Not a big fortune, but the answer to paying off our bills of such long standing.

I began to really look for the money. I prayed for it, begged for it, hoped for it. I started on a performance binge. I thought, "If I'm a real good girl, pray hard and correctly, God will send the money to us." Sarah Bernhardt never worried over a performance as much as I worried over mine.

At one meeting Tricia told me about the eleventh commandment, "Don't sweat it." I felt a release for a while, but the worry kept replacing the tiny grain of faith.

We talked about Jesus, the Holy Spirit and all that. I was familiar with the words and I thought maybe I was a Christian but I still wasn't sure what a Christian was. I didn't feel anything. I was so insecure.

At the same time I was also having a lot of trouble with love. I thought that I should love everyone but there were just some people I couldn't love, or even like, and I felt guilty. I decided since I didn't even like myself much I shouldn't be bothered about not loving others. When I shared that with Tricia one day she hit the ceiling and immediately came over with a copy of Peter Gillquist's book, *Love Is Now*.

That book contained the key that unlocked the door I had been trying to pry open for so long. As I read and reread I began to realize not only in my mind but in my spirit, that I was already an heiress. I was entitled to all that belongs to the Father, NOW! Not next week, or next month, or next year, or in the sweet bye-and-bye, but NOW! All I had to do was claim my inheritance.

Now I began to be free. Now I knew I was forgiven, past, present and future. Now I knew eternal life was a present possession. Now I had all I needed but none of it depended on anything I did.

I began to see and experience that my performance had nothing to do with my standing with God. I was set free. Free from having to keep climbing that old ladder whose rungs kept breaking with each struggling step.

I feel relaxed now in my relationship with God. I'm not struggling anymore. I just enjoy each day, experiencing the facts that love is NOW and that all He has for me is NOW.

I can't tell you the day or hour I became a Christian but now I know I am. Jesus Christ lives within me. He is my hope, my joy, my intercessor, my advocate, my awareness, my life and my reality.

9

"... And Thy House"

It was one of those rare winter evenings. A thousand stars penetrated the velvet black of the crisp, chill night. The busy arterial, filled with cars of Christmas shoppers double-filing home, melded into the residential boulevard that wound along the bluff overlooking the ice-gray waters of the bay.

"Only two shopping days till Christmas," thought Theresa as she and Chet drove along the quiet street on their annual Christmas gift delivery route.

"Peace on earth, good will to men." The spacious lawns were gaily bedecked with evergreens strewn with multicolored lights. Here and there a bare-

74

branched tree sported a festoon of white or blue lights, lending a stark beauty to its naked limbs. An occasional Santa perched jauntily by a chimney, holding promises of goodies yet to come.

Theresa was contented—yet not quite. Chet was so quiet, so removed this evening. Things were probably rough at work again, Theresa mused. Year-end and all that.

They rode on in silence. Then Chet spoke, "I went to see our attorney today about a divorce, Theresa."

A divorce? Stunned, Theresa felt her jaw drop. A divorce?

"This isn't any snap decision, you know," Chet continued. "I've been thinking about a divorce for a long time but I just got up the nerve to do something about it."

Theresa said nothing. She felt herself stiffen, grow numb.

Finally she felt for her voice. "Us? A divorce? But why, Chet?" She sounded foreign, distant as she spoke. Surely this wasn't she, this wasn't Chet. This terrible scene must be happening somewhere else—and to someone else—surely not to them.

She thought of their five boys. Biff, their youngest, had called after them as they left this evening, "Hurry back, Mom, Dad. Then we can make some popcorn!" There's so much at stake, Chet.

Chet was speaking. "—I'm planning on moving into an apartment tomorrow. That way I can be free to discover what life is all about."

Theresa and Chet had married young and then

in close succession had come the five boys. There really hadn't been any time to analyze, to discover what made life tick. They were too busy living it. And, of course, Chet had been engrossed in becoming an established engineer. He operated as if success was in direct proportion to how far you were able to claw your way up the ladder. During the past twenty years of their marriage he had attained a height that one might envy.

Though he was gauged by his associates as very successful and his income also indicated it, Chet had found that success, according to his own terms, and satisfaction weren't synonymous. He had arrived, only to discover that up close the scene wasn't what he had pictured it would be from a distance. There had to be more to life than this and Chet had to be free to hunt it out.

The months that followed were for Theresa the embodiment of everything she had ever feared. She again felt rejection, her greatest enemy. She thought of earlier rejection. . . .

Wayward and incorrigible. Recalcitrant. I had run away from home at thirteen. The court finally found me in a large city about a hundred miles from home living with an old man in a cheap hotel.

Rejection first plagued me two years before this when Dad died. Our family consisted of three daughters and I had become Dad's "boy." Together we would tramp over the ranch to lay irrigation pipes or saw up boards to build a chicken coop. We never talked much but there was that silent communication that needed no words.

Mother took on three jobs to take up the slack in our income when Dad was gone and this left little or no homelife for me. I was transplanted from the field into the kitchen but I never took. Cooking and such were as foreign to me as working the ranch would have been to my sisters.

After two years of trying to fit I decided to strike out on my own. I took Mother's Social Security check—I have often wondered since what they lived on that month—cashed it and ran off to find, or to lose, myself in the big city.

That's where the court found me. And labelled me. Since I didn't work out at home, and since my family was Catholic, I was assigned by court to a convent.

When I arrived at the Villa of the Sacred Heart, I had already mapped my strategy. Since I was miserable I would do all in my power to make everyone else as unhappy as possible. I suddenly became completely dependent on others for every one of my needs and could do nothing for myself. I had to be led from one place to another, bathed and fed. I wet my pants. Since I got the biggest response when I would wet on the red velvet cushion on the piano stool, I made this my usual target. I couldn't be trusted alone for I had become very destructive. I soon earned the distinction of terrifying everyone. I had been known to rip off my clothes and pull out great handfuls of hair as a result of my flagrant temper. In class I always was placed under Mother Superior's nose, for the protection of all involved.

The patience of the sisters was a tribute to the

power of God, but after a year and a half of me they decided something had to be done. From all appearances I was severely retarded. I put on a very convincing show. So convincing, in fact, that they ran me through a battery of psychological tests to determine how retarded I actually was. Then they could place me in the most appropriate custodial care.

I always had enjoyed tests. They gave me a chance to fight back at something I could see and I always came out the victor. This was to prove to be the chink in my armor. I scored abnormally high on all the tests—so high that I was put through the whole series again for there must have been a mistake—and was forced to admit that my imbecilic posture was a farce.

The following day I was summoned into Mother Katherine's office.

"Theresa, from now on, I'm going to level with you. You almost got away with your act, but you should know that the court confined you here until you are eighteen years of age or until you graduate from our high school."

The way she played her hand she must have known that three more years like the past eighteen months looked awfully grim to me. At that point I decided to change tactics, to beat them at their own game. No one ever studied harder than I. No one ever attempted to fit the model-pupil mold more than myself. At the end of the three years that followed, I graduated valedictorian of my class with all the honors one could wish to receive.

I decided to use the new Theresa to buy my

mother's love. Whenever I would write home, I would tear off the grades from the top of my papers—A, A-, Excellent—and enclose these little bits of paper with my letters as an offering to appease the rejection. But when Mother wrote, once every six months or so, no comment was ever made about my achievements.

Finally graduation day came. At last my family would have to recognize me and be proud. I had it all planned out. I saw in my mind's eye the chapel filled with parents and guests. My mother and sisters would sit in the very front, beaming with pride as I led my class down the aisle to receive our diplomas. I saw Mother's smile as they read off the honors I received. I felt her embrace as she put her arm around me and told me how pleased she was.

But that's not the way it happened. Instead, I was called into Mother Superior's office shortly before the service to be told that my mother had just called and that she wouldn't be coming to get me.

Terror gripped me. Not coming to get me? If no one came for me, I could never leave. Why, there was a woman here that was fifty-three years old. No one had ever come to get her when she graduated, or ever since. Terror yielded to despair.

I was all prepared to go through the motions that afternoon even though I knew that graduation wouldn't mean my freedom. I steeled myself and filed up to the altar with my classmates. As we were receiving our diplomas my eyes ran over the crowd of proud parents and friends. Suddenly a twinkling eye caught mine. And a smile. My uncle! My no-good, mentally deranged—according to family rumors—uncle! Someone cared enough to come for me!

So I went home and began to look for a job. I sent a resumé to the local bank and called for an interview.

When I went in for my appointment the bank manager laughed. I couldn't understand—he had been so impressed with my credentials.

"You sitting in the front office? Why, you'd scare all the depositors away!"

For the first time, I saw myself as I really was. One hundred ninety-two pounds, fifty-seven-inch hips, glasses with lenses as thick as bottle glass, and wall-to-wall acne topped by a Dutch bob haircut. In the convent they don't teach you everything.

So I turned to the only acceptance I had ever found. I got a job as a secretary in a Catholic nursing home. . . .

On Theresa's birthday, Chet moved out of their home into an apartment. The loneliness and the emptiness that filled the house in his absence preyed upon her. She had to get busy.

A neighbor in the next block heard about Theresa and invited her to a prayer group at her home. The friendliness and acceptance of these people gave Theresa a sense of belonging, of being wanted. She started on a prayer group circuit, one every morning and one at night.

"And everywhere I asked people to pray for me, to pray for Chet to come home. I didn't ask for myself. Who was I to think that God should listen to me?"

In an attempt to bridge the financial gap, Theresa began to look for a job. She had heard enough and seen enough at the prayer groups she attended to know that there must be a God. She still seriously doubted that He would care for her.

One day in rebellion and challenge she shook her fist at Him.

"Okay, if You're there and if You care, get me a job!"

The neighborhood paper came out that afternoon and Theresa checked the ads. A lawyer needed a housekeeper to come in every morning to clean and the pay sounded great. She called. The job was so tailor-made for her situation that she couldn't doubt but what God had answered.

Every morning she would send her boys off to school and then go to her job. And every morning when she arrived, KBIQ would be on. She began to listen as she worked, and heard about "People Who Care."

One morning she called.

She was put in touch with Joan and they met for lunch the following day. Over a pizza Theresa poured out her story and told Joan of the torment of the past few months. She told her of how people had prayed for her and how recently she even had drawn up enough courage to begin asking for herself.

"Theresa, are you related to God?" Joan asked.

That stumped Theresa. What was Joan getting at?

Joan explained that through Jesus Theresa could be God's own child and heir to all He possessed.

"Asking God for something when He isn't your Father is rather presumptuous. It's like going next door and asking for five dollars. You might get it, but you'd stand a much better chance if you asked someone from your own family."

So Theresa was adopted into God's family. And things began to happen.

Somewhere Theresa heard a verse out of the Bible: "Believe on the Lord Jesus Christ, and thou shalt be saved, and thy house."

And thy house? And thy house! Was this God's promise to put her family back together, as well as herself? Even Chet?

From all indications, it was. Because of the change in their mother, the boys began to take an interest in the prayer meetings she sttended. Soon they were all going as a family. Even Alex.

Alex and his mother had a special thing going—a feud. There never seemed to be a point on which they could agree. Every issue on which Theresa would take a side, Alex would automatically take the other. And vice versa. But Alex's curiosity got the better of him—he just had to find out what was so fascinating about a prayer meeting. He went with Theresa once and then again and again. Then on his own. The kids that went—and there were lots of them—were neat and had such a good time. And he really seemed to fit.

Before long, a group of guys started dropping by the house.

"Hey, Al, how about cutting out for a swim?"

"We're going out for hamburgers, Al. Wanna come along?"

The friendship of these kids and the love in the group was just what Alex needed. If this was God, he wanted to be in on the "in" thing.

Then came Biff.

"How do you know if Jesus will take care of you, Mama?" he said one night in the car on the way home from a group.

"Ask Him to, Biff," Theresa replied.

"Okay."

And Biff was a new boy. The change in his behavior bore this out. Always a loving child, he exhibited a new kind of abandonment, a new freedom. He was quicker to laugh, quicker to tease. More secure.

God had other ideas for Jon too.

"Look at the kind of reading I do these days, Mom," Jon said one evening after dinner as he flashed a pocket edition of the New Testament for her to see. He was due to go into the army in a few days.

"What's that?" Theresa replied caustically. "Your bullet-proof vest?" She often experienced God's "invisible shield" around her—how else could she explain the fact that for the first two weeks after she met Christ she had run into only Christians? And she had told the boys about His protection. But it was nothing to joke about. She resented Jon, who had always been so sarcastic, making fun of God.

"No, Ma," sighed Jon impatiently, "I READ it. And these too." He shuffled through the cards he had taken out of his shirt pocket. Theresa saw that there was a Bible verse on each one. "Judy gave them to me. And Mr. Murray gave me the Bible. He's the neat teacher I told you about—the one who really cares about kids. He makes God sound cool. Mr. Murray's cutting classes to spend the morning with me before I leave for basic training."

So God cared about Jon. And enough, too, for Theresa that He would assure her of His love for her oldest son.

Theresa already knew that God loved Lyle. She had known it for a long time. How else would you explain the fact that he was still alive? Lyle, who had been born with a congenital heart defect and caused Theresa many anxious days as she watched the tiny newborn struggle for existence. Lyle had been hospitalized once for the diagnostic work-up that precedes heart surgery only to come down with pneumonia which cancelled any possibility of keeping his appointment with the operating room. Lyle's surgery was rescheduled in time for him to recover from pneumonia and come down with a case of the measles the day he was to be readmitted.

The anguish of those days had been horrendous. Theresa remembered going up to the hospital to see Lyle. He was only three at the time, and his little red tricycle had been admitted with him. He would mount the trike and tear down the hall, nurses and doctors stepping quickly aside for the "fastest wheel in the West." And then he would begin to tire. Theresa could see him even now, lips a little blue, panting, hopping off the tricycle and squatting on the floor, resting his chin in his hands, his elbows on his knees. This was the way Nature taught him to recoup enough to declare another siege on the hospital corridor.

When his surgery had been cancelled twice, Theresa gave up—to God. Where else was there to turn? Three more times Lyle's doctors rescheduled the surgery, only to cancel for various reasons— Lyle's growing too fast, Lyle's got a cold. Finally, Lyle seems to be doing better so let's wait and see.

So they waited. Meanwhile, Lyle grew into a strapping lad of six-foot three who could best any and all of his brothers in a wrestling match on the living room rug.

One night on the way home from a football game, Lyle stopped by to pick up his mom at—you guessed it—a prayer meeting. The meeting was almost over. He stopped to talk with one of the men there.

"Mom sure is different since she's been coming to all these prayer meetings. Even the house is different. I guess God must have moved in. I like it this way. Think I might even give God a try."

God performed heart surgery too. Only His was a little more extensive.

Eddie sensed a difference in things around home too. He started tagging along to all Theresa's meetings. To watch him in the group was something beautiful to behold. It was almost as if a door to his soul had been opened. Love and peace found expression as they poured out. Eddie had found his element.

But God wasn't to stop with Theresa's immediate

family. "And thy house" had much broader connotations.

Jan, Theresa's sister, came West for a visit. But not to visit Theresa. She had met a man from Seattle at work and decided to "look him up as long as she was in town." Shortly after she arrived at Theresa's she called him. He would be delighted to see her. How would she like to do the town?

She would, of course, and hurried to get dressed. She sat down in the living room to wait. And wait. And wait. Joe never did come.

Nor did he come the next night. Jan had called him the following afternoon and they again made plans for the evening, but they didn't materialize.

So Jan, heartbroken at being "stood up" her first two nights in town, tearfully went to the prayer meeting that night with Theresa. "All dressed up and no place to go" or a prayer meeting—what a choice!

And it was just as much a bore as she had predicted. But what do you do when you're socially stranded in a strange town? She went back with Theresa the next night and the next. Then she began to listen. Why these people actually thought God was alive! And the stories they told about Him in action lent support to their beliefs. Supposing she gambled on God and gave Him her life? What would happen? Having nothing to lose and everything to gain, she took the chance—and found He was all they said He was. The rest of Jan's time in Seattle was everything you could ever ask of a vacation—people fun to be with, people fun to be one with.

Then it came time to leave for the long drive home. How Theresa dreaded letting her go! Who would take care of her? It would be a real comedown after dwelling under the protective umbrella of Christian love for the past two weeks.

But Theresa's fears were groundless. Her "invisible shield" was contagious. The first person Jan talked to after she got out of her car when she reached home was a Christian. She was taken promptly into the shelter of His love.

But Jan was soon forced to face the reality of the world-as-usual the first day back at work. She was welcomed home to the office with the news that her job was being phased out. A letter of termination lay on her desk. Hello and good-bye.

So back to the want ads. God knew and God cared. She checked off the few jobs available—this was a college town and there were more people than there was work—and began her hunt. One job looked particularly promising. But no, it was expecting too much. Having only a high school education and having to compete with all the college students on the job market kept you from shooting too high. But I might as well try them all, she told herself. Even the good one.

That evening, Jan unlocked the door of her apartment, sat down on the couch and kicked off her shoes—victorious! In less than twenty-four hours she had been fired and hired. The new job— the one she never thought she could get—was a real step up. What had Theresa said? Oh, yes. "My God shall supply all your needs."

Theresa's "invisible shield" was not only for her

protection but for others as well. Nor was it always invisible.

Late one evening a business associate who had sold cleaning products with Theresa some time ago called and asked if he could come over. The company had a new sales promotion out, he said, and he wanted her to see it. Could he come over? That would be fine, Theresa replied. And proper. The boys were all home.

But the hour grew later and the man didn't appear. Finally, about eleven o'clock, the door bell rang and there was Mr. James.

They sat at the kitchen table and Theresa poured them each a cup of coffee.

"Another cup?"

"Please."

The sales promotion was never mentioned. Finally, about 2:00 A.M. and several pots of coffee later, Mr. James brought up the subject of "religion."

"I hear you got religion, Theresa."

Theresa smiled. "I don't know about that, Paul," she said, "but I did find God and His love and He's everything I could have hoped for."

"They say you've been running around to all these kooky prayer meetings and that you're different. Maybe that explains why I felt spooked when I came up to the door tonight. I waited until I thought your sons would all be asleep before I came. I figured that since your husband had been gone for so long that you would be lonely and a real pushover. When I came up your front steps, I wanted to turn around and run for some reason. I had the funny feeling that my plans wouldn't come out quite like I thought. I hadn't counted on God."

Theresa told Paul of the incredible protection afforded her by God since he had become her Bodyguard. Paul listened intently.

Finally, at 4:00 A.M., Paul rose to leave. There was a smile in his eye and a new sense of direction in his voice as he spoke.

"I had been feeling like a failure and thought a conquest would give me a sense of power and put me on my feet. But now I know real Power. I can hardly wait to tell my wife!"

He did go home to tell his wife. Together, they talked the rest of the night. The next day they started off in a new direction together.

Theresa's housekeeping job was a real source of satisfaction to her during the first few months that Chet was gone. The lawyer for whom she worked was a fine Christian man who understood thoroughly what she was going through. If he were still home when she arrived, they would have a cup of coffee together before he left. In time Theresa told him about her marital situation and how she wished Chet would come home.

"You would take him back after he ran out on you and the boys? Only God could make a person that forgiving!"

And then, "You know, my wife ran out on me a few years ago. She's told me often how wrong she was and how sorry she is still. I couldn't find it in myself to forgive her. But God could make me that forgiving. I should let her come home."

"Blessed be the God that comforts us so that we may be able to comfort others." Soon Theresa got word that the lawyer and his wife were looking to-gether for a new home in which to start over.

God has made a decided difference in Theresa's life. There are still ups and downs but now she doesn't have to endure them alone.

Not long ago, Theresa stormed at God, "Why? Why did you have to take Chet away?"

As if He had spoken the words inside her head, Theresa heard:

"Well, I had to get your attention somehow!"

God-in-residence in Theresa has its effects on Chet too. He commented to her one evening when he came to visit the boys, "Where are all your wrinkles?"

"I guess I don't have them anymore," she laughed. "I'm so happy now. God's my Friend, you know."

"Well, maybe I wouldn't mind believing in a God like that," Chet said thoughtfully. Chet, who had previously told her to shut up every time she mentioned God. Chet, the self-imposed atheist, or at best, an agnostic.

Theresa still is waiting for God to bring Chet home. She lives with the possibility, though, that her desires might never materialize. But she says, "I'm happy. I have found this past year that it is possible, though not pleasant, to live without my husband. I know now that I could never live without God."

10
Not Guilty

"Wendy, you'd be so pretty if you'd only lose some weight."

"Oh Mom, how many times have you said that to me?"

"I just hate to see you waste your life away. If I didn't love you I wouldn't say anything."

Wendy quietly slipped into her room, her hazel eyes swelling with tears. Who really cares anyway, she wondered as she gathered her cat, Toby, into her arms. Toby didn't care that Wendy was fat. He didn't make her measure up to a price tag of performance.

She cradled the cat in her arms a long time. He was important to Wendy. From him she felt the acceptance that she hadn't found in any human. The cat couldn't return her love though. Not really, and Wendy felt an emptiness.

As she sat holding her fluffy bundle of security, she scribbled a poem as she often did in moments of frustration. . . .

. . . . And tomorrow is come.
Patience waits another time.
Perhaps one day soon. . . .

"Yes, one day," she reflected, "I'll know what it's all about."

Being home from college was not so great. Oh, it was refreshing to be back at her piano, to have this emotional outlet and to be doing something creative. Wendy loved music. But then there was the strain of trying to please her parents, especially Mother. There were always the subtle and not-so-subtle remarks about her weight. Wendy just couldn't measure up to her mother's standards for her. She was relieved when it was time to go back to the dorm with the other girls. . . .

"Wendy," came a familiar wail.

"I'm here," she replied from her room, knowing by the voice it was Joan.

"If you can't guess I'll be disappointed up to my eyeballs. Go on, guess what happened."

Wendy gazed at her brimming friend and teased, "Ole knobby knees decided you deserved an 'A' on that test yesterday."

"Come on, Wendy," Joan urged. "This is big news."

Knowing all the time the reason for Joan's excitement she refused to let on. "I know," she mused,

"Pete looked at you and then dreamily gazed into your baby blues and whispered tenderly: 'Hey, you smell like a pineapple!' "

"Oh, Wendy, you're impossible," Joan impatiently implored. "Be serious."

"All right, *he* asked you out."

"Right," Joan murmured and pretended to swoon on the bed. "Thank God for beautiful men," and with that she fluttered out the door. "Tell you the details later. Gotta study now."

"Bye," Wendy answered and settled down to study herself. But as she read, printed word tumbled into troubled thought. Thank God for . . . thank God . . . God . . . Oh yes, that spirit whose presence was as remote as that boy she kept dreaming about or that place she longed to belong to. What did God have to do with anything anyway? Yet she had heard once in church that He was attainable and that He cared. Really cared. Wendy was skeptical about that. If God was for real and He cared, why was she so confused? So empty? So lonely?

Days marched into months and things began to change in Wendy's life. Studies and thoughts of God became secondary as she became preoccupied with other matters.

For the first time in her twenty-two years Wendy was dating. And more, she belonged to a group of students who cared more for each other than about what people thought. It was a group of "misfits," at least from the standpoint of the "establishment" crowd. They were all different, not "Greek" material. There Wendy found acceptance. They didn't

93

mind that she was overweight. They accepted her just like she was. She could kick off her shoes, let down her hair and be herself. The group did everything together. They sang together, ate together, played together and sometimes studied together.

These friends became the center of Wendy's world. The one she cherished the most was Jason. A compassionate fellow with strong convictions for helping others. But Jason had an incurable disease that promised him less than a year to live.

Soon Jason became more than a friend. Wendy wasn't sure whether what she found herself feeling for Jason was love, infatuation or pity. But her feelings for him deepened as their relationship continued. It wasn't long before Wendy found herself giving herself completely to Jason. Morals were discarded as obsolete. Mother's religious and moral training was left in the past to be replaced by the desire to please and to make Jason's last year a happy year for him.

At last Wendy felt needed, appreciated, important.

All too soon summer came. School, friends, parties and the group came to an end. Wendy went home again a little older, perhaps a little wiser, but more confused than ever.

Wendy's grades had reflected her preoccupation and to her utter disappointment she learned she could not return to school in the fall.

She took a job as a secretary that was deplorable to her, but at least it was a job. She got an apartment with a girl friend and existed on work and memories. The promised letters from her friends back at school, even Jason, didn't come and loneliness enveloped her.

She missed her piano and on weekends when she went home she would empty out her frustrations on the keyboard where she sat for hours on end.

Alone one night she began to think about who she was, what she was, where she was going. She thought of her chastity that she had traded for acceptance and love. Now it was only a memory. And not even a happy memory because the pain of loneliness was far greater. A sense of guilt hovered over her, filled her with remorse, dragged her down until she wished she could die. If only there was someone she could talk to, someone who would understand. But there was no one.

January came and with it an awareness that Wendy was twenty-three and still going nowhere. Most girls her age were married or educated and working at a profession.

The realization of her predicament hit her one night as she listened to strains of music on her radio. She was so alone and life seemed so futile. Then a voice intruded into her thoughts, a voice from the radio. He said something about God caring for a person, that He wanted to relieve loneliness. "God cares about me?" she thought as she listened for another word of promise. She reflected on the words she had heard and began to write . . .

> Oh, It's cold out here.
> Please Lord, let me come in.
> Show me the way to your world . . .

In the days that followed that voice from the

radio continued to haunt her. The voice that said there was someone who cared, someone to help her right now. Now! If there was release from this desperate plight, now was the time to get it. But she hesitated. She didn't want a sermon or a lecture on morals and sin, though she was prepared for it. What she really needed was someone to listen and to care. But who would listen without judgment? The voice persisted.

A few weeks later on a Sunday night when Wendy's roommate was gone she heard that voice again. "God cares and forgives." Forgives? "Call now." She scribbled the phone number hastily on a scrap of paper. Trembling, she dialed the number.

That night Wendy blurted her story out to Vickie over the phone. Her guilt and her loneliness came pouring out. Wendy felt a little better. She needed a friend and was eager to meet with Vickie over coffee the following evening. She filled Vickie in on all the details. Vickie wasn't shocked or horrified as Wendy had expected. She listened with interest and compassion as Wendy talked for an hour and a half. Vickie was even able to identify with Wendy's story. She shared some of her own experiences with her then told her about Jesus. Not the distant, indifferent Jesus of the Sunday morning worship service. Not the Jesus lying in a manger celebrated at Christmas time. Not the meek and mild lifeless portrait hanging on the wall. Wendy had been brought up in the church with all of its religiosity. Though she hadn't given up religion, at twenty-three she had not experienced any reality in it and had abandoned any hope of that.

But this Jesus she was hearing about was something else. Alive today. Having paid the penalty for all of Wendy's shortcomings over 2,000 years ago. And most of all He wasn't taking into account anything she had done. The price had been paid on the cross. Wendy was forgiven for every sin she had ever committed, past, present and even future. He had not only provided her with permanent forgiveness and eternal life for the asking, He wanted to fill that vacancy in her life with Himself. Wendy could actually begin to live by the life of God. All she had to do was receive it.

When they parted that night, Wendy thanked Vickie and told her that was the first time in her life anyone had ever listened to her. It was such a relief to find someone who cared enough to just listen and not have a lot of pat answers.

The following evening Wendy showed up at Vickie's house where a small group met weekly. She prayed right out loud in the meeting. "Oh God, thank you for Jesus. Thank you for your forgiveness. Thank you for giving your life to me and for these 'People Who Care'."

You couldn't keep Wendy away from the group after that. She came every week and sparkled with new life.

She found a job in a rest home. It was just perfect for her. Again she felt worthwhile, needed. She loved to cheer up the old people. It was a challenge but Wendy delighted in it. Her radiant smile captured their hearts, but Wendy gave Jesus all the credit and she didn't mind telling them Who it was that gave her this new quality of life.

And then there was the day her thirteen-year-old sister wandered into Wendy's room. "Wendy," she said, "you're different. How can I have Jesus in my life?"

11
Help Wanted

Barbara eased her car into the freeway traffic and headed south. The green fields, bright with morning dew, were interrupted only by the staccato of pasture fences.

A promise of a fine day. That she had just finished the eleven to seven shift a few hours previously didn't erase the wonder of this day. It had been a long time in coming.

As she pulled into the inside lane and began to pick up speed, the events that brought this special day into being came to her—finishing her B.S. degree in nursing, working night shift in that nursing home, and, oh yes—that radio station.

Barbara had happened upon KBIQ one day when her son, Dan, was gone for the weekend and Robert was out of town. She had turned on the radio while tidying up the apartment and twirled the dial until she found some listenable music. Every now and then the programming was interrupted by a sneaky little religious comment, and she began to listen. She knew what the man was talking about. She had been exposed to church—Daddy had dropped her off at Sunday School every week and she had been very active in Christian Endeavor. But what the announcer was talking about seemed personal. She listened for the next "God commercial."

Barbara turned on the station regularly after that to hear what the man might have to say about God. She disagreed with some of what she heard, but other things caused her to think about Jesus Christ and her own life.

She started bombarding Robert with all sorts of questions. Was there a God? What was He like? What did life mean? In all the four years they had been seeing each other they had never talked with any seriousness about anything bordering on religion.

Barbara signalled, then moved over into the outside lane, readying for the exit. The sun was just breaking through the early morning haze. Bright spurs of yellow forsythia stretched into the gray, reaching for the warmth of spring. The lavender and white crocuses dotted the random plots of newly turned brown sod. Remnants of the cold November afternoon when she had first driven out to Kings Garden were nowhere to be found.

She had been working the night when she ran

across the ad. A lull in that evening's routine had given her time to thumb through the paper and the words stood out of the help-wanted column:

NURSING HOME
Director of Nursing Service
Dedicated to Christian Service
Bachelor of Science in Nursing Required

Soon after Barbara had started to listen to the "fishhooks" on the radio she had bought a Bible, hoping to find answers to the questions she found in her mind. She had decided to search on her own rather than call the phone number given so frequently on the air. She began to use every spare minute in her search and started to bring her Bible to work, taking it out to read when she had a break. She talked with people with whom she worked about what she was reading, constantly asking questions. Still, what did the "Dedicated to Christian Service" mean, she wondered.

Yet, the ad was intriguing and the position looked promising. Her curiosity won out and she called and made an appointment with Mr. Miles the administrator.

Dan had driven out with her the day she went for the first appointment. They spotted the sign, "Kings Garden," and turned off the street at the entrance. A tree-lined boulevard, flanked on either side by carpets of green lawn and carefully tended shrubbery, led past the many neat buildings to an imposing brick building that would have been the envy of any college campus. The structure towered far above the surrounding evergreens, lending a quiet dignity to its environment. Barbara read the signs on the buildings as she drove past: *Senior Citizens Community, Retirement Apartments, Gift Shop, Grade School, High School* and *KBIQ Radio.* So KBIQ was part of this too!

She spotted the nursing home. Mr. Miles had said that construction had begun on new quarters. Barbara could see the gray concrete foundation and the skeleton of framework etched against the chill winter sky.

Barbara had liked Mr. Miles the moment they met. His casual, disarming smile put her at ease. But the skeptic in her responded, "He seems so genuine, so sincere, what's the catch?"

Yet the longer they talked, the more real Mr. Miles seemed. He appeared interested in Barbara as a person rather than just as personnel. When he asked why she had answered the ad, she was left stumbling for a response. He told her that the nursing home was just part of the complex she had witnessed when she had driven in. He asked about her experience with God.

She had had nothing to say. So Mr. Miles took two little white booklets out of his desk and handed one to her. As they looked through them, he explained that God had a specific plan for her individual life. Barbara listened and read on ahead. She saw that they would soon come to a place where she would have to make a decision about turning her life over to Christ.

"If he asks me to respond to this challenge here and now, I'll turn on my heel and never come back again!" she promised herself.

But when Mr. Miles got to that part of the booklet, he smiled and closed it.

"Well, Barbara," he had said, "That's what it's all about."

At the end of the interview, Mr. Miles had said, "Go home and pray about the job."

Pray? She hadn't prayed for so long. She told him that she didn't think she knew how.

"You'll know how," he replied as she rose to leave.

When she had returned to the car Dan had wanted to know all about the interview, the job and the administrator. He was her oldest son from a previous marriage, and delighted in assuming a paternal role in her life. They were good friends. He had told her when they talked about the job that he thought that "it might do you some good."

"Dan," she had responded to all his questions, "That isn't a job; it's a way of life."

Barbara pulled into a parking spot near the new nursing home. The forms and foundations of eighteen months ago had grown into three-storied contemporary buildings. The piles of dirt had been replaced with azaleas already budding with the promise of an early summer.

She approached the receptionist's desk.

"I'm Mrs. Sorenson. I have a ten o'clock appointment with Mr. Miles."

She took a chair, and began to leaf through a magazine.

Eighteen months ago she would never have guessed that she would be here today. She had often thought about the job after that first interview and thought even more about God. But a short time later she and Robert had married—that was a story in itself!—and moved to a neighboring town where he was finishing college in order to become a teacher.

Their orginal plans had included a move to Alaska when Robert graduated this June, but no openings had turned up and they had contacted every major school board in the state. Maybe God had a better idea.

"Mr. Miles will see you now." The receptionist smiled at her.

Barbara made her way through the open door. Mr. Miles rose from his desk and shook her hand warmly.

"It's so good to see you again," he said. "Tell me why you're here."

So Barbara told him of the job hunt, and how, in turning over every possibility, she and Robert had turned their lives over to God so He could put them where He wanted them.

"Then I found your ad again in the evening paper, and took this to be His green light."

Mr. Miles smiled, and looked up. "Eighteen months is a long time to go without a nursing director. Earlier this morning I had an appointment scheduled with the woman I had decided to hire for the position. Something came up, though, and she had to cancel."

Barbara took the job at Kings Garden. But that was not the end. It was a means to the end that she might come to know Jesus Christ and experience His best for her.

12

The People Who Care

In the preceding chapters you, the reader, have been introduced to many of the individuals who have responded to "People Who Care." With few exceptions, they have chosen to retain their true names in the stories they have unfolded because, as one put it, "I've tried to tell many of my friends what Christ has done for and with me. If they see me in print then they might sit up and take notice." (Those who have chosen to assume another identity have done so in order to protect the other people involved in their story.)

And in the process of meeting these people you have also met many of the "People Who Care." In regard to them one might say, "Only the names have been changed to protect the innocent." But when one personality touches another, innocence—or uninvolvement—must go.

"People Who Care" are essentially just that—people who care first about God and therefore about others. They hesitate to refer to themselves as "counselors." All thirteen of them are lay people and they have found that the term, "counselor," gives the connotation of psychologist, social worker or professional marriage counselor. And the people with whom they talk often feel a need for personal rather than a professional contact.

The "People Who Care" come from diverse backgrounds. Take, for example, the case of Allan and Sandy. (Again, the names have been changed.) Married just out of high school, they came to Christ seven years ago from a background of social, bordering dangerously on problem, drinking and the party life. Jesus so radically changed their life that they found they had no further need for the pacifying props of their pre-Christian existence. In finding stability in Christ, and subsequently in themselves and in their marriage, their new life spilled over onto others who in turn responded to the Author of the new life.

And then meet Gordon and Jenny. Both raised in fine Christian homes, they responded to Christ early in their lives. When they married, they both determined that Christ was to be the head of their new corporation. As in the Mosaic Law they were careful to teach the precepts of the Faith to their children. They were privileged to be part not only of the births of their offspring but also of their re-births. Yet their responsibility did not end when they drove out their driveway. They met other people who needed their hope too.

God's programming is always ideal. His "better idea" necessitates a variety of people. He always matches those who call with one of His own who can identify with that person. A nurse will call in when one of the "People Who Care," who just happens to be a nurse, is on. A man at the edge of divorce will invariably call the night an Allan is on. One woman under psychiatric care was put in touch with the person on call who had been seen through a great emotional upheaval by The Great Psychiatrist. She passed her hope on to the caller. A teenager called "People Who Care" at a time when Joan, a housewife who had worked specifically with teenagers before her marriage, was taking calls.

Let it not be said that the "People Who Care" operate completely from an altruistic, self-sacrificing motive. The richness brought into their own lives by the friendships of those who call in and the miracles they are privileged to experience as God touches those with whom they speak more than compensates for any inconvenience that they might incur.

The friendships that result from a person in crisis reaching out for a point of solidarity are spiritual therapy not only for the one that reaches but also for the one they touch. As the person who calls is put into contact with the truest Friend, an allegiance often forms with the one who introduces them. Two people striking a note of response within each other is a healing thing.

A young woman, after one phone conversation with one of the "People," wrote a song as a gift to show her appreciation. The gift was delivered complete with guitar when they met in person for the first time:

> Can I say I like you,
> And can I say—Thank you,
> For accepting me.
> We all need a good friend—
> Wouldn't you agree?
>
> Who is your friend?
> Friends are never earned.
> Finding a friend is a rare—
> But important—thing.
> They are a gift from the loving God
> And are precious.
>
> Who is your friend?
> Is he there when you need him—
> And does he care?
>
> So can I say I like you
> And can I say—Thank you,
> For accepting me,
> My good friend.

Who's to say who benefits the most?

The story of "People Who Care" is just beginning. God continues to add chapter upon chapter as He unfolds His plan for His children. The setting of the story has begun to take on international proportions. Concerned people in Los Angeles, Chicago and even Central and South America are at work writing God's story upon the lives of individuals in their cities and countries through a "People Who Care" approach to helping others.

More information about this novel method that God is using to make Himself heard may be obtained by writing the originator of "People Who Care":

Mr. Phill Butler
P.O. Box 9323
Seattle, Washington 98109